The War of Words

POCKET HISTORY

The War of Words

History's great military speeches, songs, war cries & final words

James Inglis

CONTENTS

Introduction
Winning Hearts & Minds **8**

The Death of Pisander in the Trojan War,
From Homer, The Iliad, *c. 750 BC* **10**

The Fall of Miletus, 494 BC
From Herodotus, The Histories, *c. 440 BC* **16**

Catiline Prepares for Battle at Pistoria, Italy, 62 BC
From Sallust, The Conspiracy of Catiline, *43–42 BC* **22**

Boudicca Addresses Her Army, AD 60 or 61
From Tacitus, Annals, *AD 109* **25**

'Be Ye the Avengers of Noble Blood'
William the Conqueror, Hastings, England, 1066 **29**

Address at the Council of Clermont
Pope Urban, Clermont, France, 1095 **34**

Letter to King Henry VI of England
Joan of Arc, France, 1429 **40**

'I Have the Heart of a King'
Elizabeth I, Tilbury Fort, Essex, England, 1588 **45**

'Give Me Liberty, or Give Me Death!'
Patrick Henry, Richmond, United States, 1775 **49**

'We Must Dare, Dare Again, Always Dare'
Georges Jacques Danton, Paris, 1792 **56**

Farewell to the Old Guard
Napoleon Bonaparte, Paris, 1814 **60**

'To Arms, All—All of You!'
Giuseppe Garibaldi, Naples, Italy, 1860 **63**

Gettysburg Address
Abraham Lincoln, Gettysburg, United States, 1863 **66**

Last Speech
Abraham Lincoln, Washington, D.C., 1865 **69**

'I Will Fight No More Forever'
Chief Joseph, Montana, United States, 1877 **75**

The 'Four Minute Men'
Volunteer speeches, United States, 1917–18 **79**

Against Conscription & War
Emma Goldman, New York, 1917 **86**

'Germany Expected to Find a Lamb & Found a Lion'
David Lloyd George, London, 1917 **93**

Speech to the Industry Club
Adolf Hitler, Dusseldorf, Germany, 1932 **97**

'Before the Gate of Germany Stands the New German Army'
Adolf Hitler, Nuremberg, Germany, 1936 **107**

'Peace for Our Time'
Neville Chamberlain, London, 1938 **115**

Declaration of War
Robert Menzies, Canberra, Australia, 1939 **117**

Fireside Chat on the War in Europe
Franklin D. Roosevelt, Washington, D.C., 1939 **120**

Radio Address to the German People
Neville Chamberlain, London, 1939 **126**

'We Shall Never Surrender'
Winston Churchill, London, 1940 **129**

'This Was Their Finest Hour'
Winston Churchill, London, 1940 **139**

'We Are Merely Interested in Safeguarding Peace'
Adolf Hitler, Berlin, 1941 **143**

Reaction to the German Invasion of Russia
Vyacheslav Molotov, Moscow, 1941 **150**

Declaration of War on Japan
Franklin D. Roosevelt, Washington, D.C., 1941 **154**

'The Black of the Night Must Pass'
John Curtin, Canberra, Australia, 1942 **158**

Speech to the US Third Army
General George S. Patton, England, 1944 **170**

The Atom Bomb
Harry S. Truman, Potsdam, Germany, 1945 **181**

The Cuban Missile Crisis
John F. Kennedy, Washington, D.C., 1962 **185**

'Our Cause Is Just'
Margaret Thatcher, London, 1982 **193**

Attack on Iraq
George Bush Sr, Washington, D.C., 1991 **200**

'Freedom from Fear'
Rudy Giuliani, New York, 2001 **210**

'A Turning Point in History'
Tony Blair, Brighton, England, 2001 **217**

'Axis of Evil'
George W. Bush, Washington, D.C., 2002 **227**

Index **237**

INTRODUCTION

Winning Hearts & Minds

The *War of Words* shows us at our best and worst. It consists of a variety of war-related speeches, writings, songs, poems, battle cries, famous last words, short quotes and aphorisms from throughout history, arranged in chronological order. While showing how language has been used over the centuries to win support for a range of causes, it also examines the motives of the speakers, writers and composers, both stated and concealed, and highlights some of the verbal and emotional tricks they employed to further their ambitions.

Some of the texts are remarkable for their honesty, others for their duplicity. The majority are inspirational. Many are honest; many are composed of outrageous lies. Some are hilarious, often unintentionally. Sarcasm and irony are well represented, unsurprisingly. All the speakers show passion and a love of either war or peace (or, in some cases, both). There are bigoted rants designed to dehumanise, inspiring calls to arms, impassioned railings and motivational gee-ups.

As we look back into history, and around the modern world, it appears that there will be no respite from war in the foreseeable future. Perhaps this territorial disease that blights our planet is carried only by extremists, nationalists and those who hold power, for most people everywhere seem to have the same simple ambitions: to earn a living safely and peacefully while supporting their family and enjoying their friends.

Perhaps one day we will learn to sublimate the counterproductive aspects of our inherent competitiveness, and agree to settle our differences with, for instance, a sporting contest. Or a debate—that would indeed be the pinnacle of a war of words!

The Death of Pisander in the Trojan War
From Homer, The Iliad, c. 750 BC

Little is known about Homer and, in fact, many scholars believe there was no such person, and that the works attributed to him are actually collections of traditional oral poetry composed by others.

Widely held to be the oldest surviving work of Greek, and hence European, literature, *The Iliad* is an epic poem about the tenth and final year of the Greek siege of the city of Ilion during the Trojan War; the word *iliad* means 'pertaining to Ilion', the capital city of Troy, in modern-day Turkey. Some scholars believe there is a historical basis to *The Iliad*, others that Homer's stories are a fusion of different tales of wars and expeditions by Greeks during the Bronze Age (about the twelfth or eleventh centuries BC).

According to Greek mythology, the roots of the Trojan War were formed when two powerful gods, Zeus and Poseidon, tried to seduce the sea goddess Thetis. But Zeus' wife Themis warned them that any son of Thetis would inevitably usurp them and eventually rule Olympus, the Greek pantheon of the twelve major gods, so Zeus decided to marry off Thetis to Peleus, a mortal.

All the gods and goddesses were invited to the wedding except Eris, the goddess of discord and strife. Furious at this slight, Eris lobbed a golden apple, inscribed 'For the fairest', into the wedding party. Three powerful goddesses—Hera, Athena and Aphrodite—each claimed the prize, and asked Zeus to arbitrate on who was 'the fairest'. But Zeus referred the decision to Paris, a Trojan prince. Each goddess offered Paris a reward: Athena would make him a great war leader and hero, Hera promised to install him as ruler of the most powerful kingdom on earth, while Aphrodite promised him the hand in marriage of the most beautiful woman in the world—Helen, the wife of Menelaus of Sparta, who would later become known as Helen of Troy.

Paris chose Aphrodite as the fairest, thereby enraging the two most powerful goddesses in the pantheon. Helen duly fell in love with Paris, who abducted her and took her to Troy. Infuriated, for ten years the Greeks besieged Troy under the leadership of Agamemnon, the King of Mycenae, eventually achieving victory after the Trojans were duped by the Trojan Horse ruse.

In the ensuing war, the Greeks slaughtered the Trojans and desecrated their temples, thus incurring the wrath of the gods. During their journey home, the surviving Greeks, led by Odysseus (Ulysses), experienced shipwrecks, storms and other god-given disasters.

In this excerpt, Menelaus of Sparta kills the Trojan Pisander and gloats over his body. Homer makes the point that unless we apply reason and self-control to our emotions, virtuous anger can deteriorate into resentment or unmanageable rage.

Pisander then made straight at Menelaus—his evil destiny luring him on to his doom, for he was to fall in fight with you, O Menelaus. When the two were hard by one another the spear of the son of Atreus turned aside and he missed his aim; Pisander then struck the shield of brave Menelaus but could not pierce it, for the shield stayed the spear and broke the shaft; nevertheless he was glad and made sure of victory; forthwith, however, the son of Atreus drew his sword and sprang upon him. Pisander then seized the bronze battle-axe, with its long and polished handle of olive wood that hung

by his side under his shield, and the two made at one another. Pisander struck the peak of Menelaus' crested helmet just under the crest itself, and Menelaus hit Pisander as he was coming towards him, on the forehead, just at the rise of his nose; the bones cracked and his two gore-bedrabbled eyes fell by his feet in the dust. He fell backwards to the ground, and Menelaus set his heel upon him, stripped him of his armour, and vaunted over him saying:

'Even thus shall you Trojans leave the ships of the Achaeans, proud and insatiate of battle though you be; nor shall you lack any of the disgrace and shame which you have heaped upon myself. Cowardly she-wolves that you are, you feared not the anger of dread Jove, avenger of violated hospitality, who will one day destroy your city; you stole my wedded wife and wickedly carried off much treasure when you were her guest, and now you would fling fire upon our ships, and kill our heroes. A day will come when, rage as you may, you shall be stayed. O father Jove, you, who they say art above all both gods and men in wisdom, and from whom all things that befall us do proceed, how can you thus favour the Trojans—men so proud and overweening, that they are never tired of fighting? All things pall after a while—sleep, love, sweet song and stately dance—still these are things of which a man would surely have his fill rather than of battle, whereas it is of battle that the Trojans are insatiate.'

So saying Menelaus stripped the bloodstained armour from the body of Pisander, and handed it over to his men; then he again ranged himself among those who were in the front of the fight.

WAR CRIES

A war cry, or battle cry, is a shout or chant used in battle by members of the same military force. The nature and content vary, depending on whether the motive is to threaten or frighten the foe, inspire the reluctant soldier, invoke a family or tribal name, communicate to cohorts that they have assistance, promote a sense of camaraderie and strength, or call on a superior being for help.

Massed voices give an advance impression of a formidable, united fighting force. Moreover, shouting stimulates the diaphragm, and many martial arts advocate a yell at the moment of release.

Schools and sports teams all over the world use formalised and traditional war cries. The haka, the fierce war dance traditionally performed by Maori warriors, is still a feature of the All Blacks rugby team's international matches.

It is intriguing to note that the word 'slogan' derives from the Scottish Gaelic *sluagh-gairm*—*sluagh* is 'people', *gairm* 'call' or 'declaration'—which means 'gathering-cry' or, during times of war, 'war cry'. In English, the word evolved through 'slughorn' and 'sluggorne' to 'slogan'.

The Fall of Miletus, 494 BC
From Herodotus, The Histories, c. 440 BC

Not much is known about the so-called Father of History, the Greek historian Herodotus (c. 484–c. 425 BC). His aim in writing *The Histories*, a nine-volume record of his travels, was to 'prevent the great and wonderful actions of the Greeks and the Barbarians [Persians] from losing their due mead of glory; and to put on record what causes first brought them into conflict'. In the work, he reports on recent wars, especially the Greek victory in the Greco–Persian Wars of 499 to 450 BC following a Greek revolt against occupation by the Persians.

These excerpts describe the Persian attacks on the Greek stronghold of Miletus, in modern-day Turkey. The first sets out the Persians' terms for surrender: submit and 'no harm shall happen', resist and the consequences will be dire—a time-honoured tactic still used today. The second notes Herodotus' admiration for the Persian leader Alyattes' policy of not razing buildings, so that 'each time that he invaded the country he might find something to plunder'.

Book I

On the side of the barbarians the number of vessels was 600. These assembled off the coast of Milesia, while the land army collected upon the shore; but the leaders, learning the strength of the Ionian fleet, began to fear lest they might fail to defeat them, in which case, not having the mastery at sea, they would be unable to reduce Miletus, and might in consequence receive rough treatment at the hands of Darius. So when they thought of all these things, they resolved on the following course: calling together the Ionian tyrants, who had fled to the Medes for refuge when Aristagoras deposed them from their governments, and who were now in camp, having joined in the expedition against Miletus, the Persians addressed them thus:

'Men of Ionia, now is the fit time to show your zeal for the house of the king. Use your best efforts, every one of you, to detach your fellow-countrymen from the general body. Hold forth to them the promise that, if they submit, no harm shall happen to them on account of their rebellion; their temples shall not be burned, nor any of their private buildings; neither shall they be treated with greater harshness than before the outbreak. But if they refuse to yield, and determine to try the chance of a battle, threaten them with the fate which shall assuredly overtake them in that case. Tell them, when they are vanquished in fight, they shall be enslaved; their boys shall be made eunuchs, and their maidens transported to Bactra; while their country shall be delivered into the hands of foreigners.'

Thus spake the Persians. The Ionian tyrants sent accordingly by night to their respective citizens, and reported the words of the Persians; but the people were all staunch, and refused to betray their countrymen, those of each state thinking that they alone had had overtures made to them ... these events happened on the first appearance of the Persians before Miletus.

Afterwards, while the Ionian fleet was still assembled at Lade, councils were held, and speeches made by divers persons—among the rest by Dionysius, the Phocaean captain, who thus expressed himself:

'Our affairs hang on the razor's edge, men of Ionia, either to be free or to be slaves; and slaves, too, who have shown themselves runaways. Now, then, you have to choose whether you will endure hardships, and so for the present lead a life of toil, but thereby gain ability to overcome your enemies and establish your own freedom; or whether you will persist in this slothfulness and disorder, in which case I see no hope of your escaping the king's vengeance for your rebellion. I beseech you, be persuaded by me, and trust yourselves to my guidance. Then, if the gods only hold the balance fairly between us, I undertake to say that our foes will either decline a battle, or, if they fight, suffer complete discomfiture.'

Book VI

This prince [Alyattes] waged war with the Medes under Cyaxares, the grandson of Deioces, drove the Cimmerians out of Asia, conquered Smyrna, the Colophonian colony, and invaded Clazomenae. From this last contest he did not come off as he could have wished, but met with a sore defeat; still, however, in the course of his reign, he performed other actions very worthy of note, of which I will now proceed to give an account.

Inheriting from his father a war with the Milesians, he pressed the siege against the city by attacking it in the following manner. When the harvest was ripe on the ground he marched his army into Milesia to the sound of pipes and harps, and flutes masculine and feminine. The buildings that were scattered over the country he neither pulled down nor burned, nor did he even tear away the doors, but left them standing as they were. He cut down, however, and utterly destroyed all the trees and all the corn throughout the land, and then returned to his own dominions. It was idle for his army to sit down before the place, as the Milesians were masters of the sea. The reason that he did not demolish their buildings was that the inhabitants might be tempted to use them as homesteads from which to go forth to sow and till their lands; and so each time that he invaded the country he might find something to plunder.

FIGHTING WORDS

'All warfare is based on deception ... Be extremely subtle, even to the point of formlessness. Be extremely mysterious, even to the point of soundlessness. Thereby you can be the director of the opponent's fate.'
Chinese writer Sun Tzu (c. 544–496 BC), The Art of War (sixth century BC)

'In war, truth is the first casualty.'
Aeschylus, Greek playwright (525–456 BC)

'Ten soldiers wisely led will beat a hundred without a head.'
Euripides, Greek playwright and philosopher (c. 480–406 BC)

'We make war that we may live in peace.'
Aristotle, Greek philosopher (384–322 BC)

'Veni, vidi, vici.' (I came, I saw, I conquered.)
Roman leader Julius Caesar's concise report to Rome after defeating Pharnaces II at Zela in Asia Minor in just five days, in 47 BC

Catiline Prepares for Battle at Pistoria, Italy, January 62 BC
From Sallust, The Conspiracy of Catiline, 43–42 BC

Lucius Catiline (c. 108–62 BC) was a charismatic Roman senator and military general with a reputation for debauchery. He spent much of his time plotting against fellow senator Cicero. After the Senate exiled him from Rome, Catiline cobbled together an army of supporters and attempted to escape to Gaul. But at Pistoria (now Pistoia) his militia was surrounded by an enormous Roman army. Whether they fought or surrendered, death was certain. Catiline decided to fight; this is the speech he gave to his doomed troops before the battle.

I am well aware, soldiers, that words cannot inspire courage; and that a spiritless army cannot be rendered active, or a timid army valiant, by the speech of its commander. Whatever courage is in the heart of a man, whether from nature or from habit, so much will be shown by him in the field; and on him whom neither glory

nor danger can move, exhortation is bestowed in vain; for the terror in his breast stops his ears …

Whithersoever we would go, we must open a passage with our swords. I conjure you, therefore, to maintain a brave and resolute spirit; and to remember, when you advance to battle, that on your own right hands depend riches, honour and glory, with the enjoyment of your liberty and of your country. If we conquer, all will be safe; we shall have provisions in abundance, and the colonies and corporate towns will open their gates to us. But if we lose the victory through want of courage, those same places will turn against us; for neither place nor friend will protect him whom his arms have not protected. Besides, soldiers, the same exigency does not press upon our adversaries, as presses upon us; we fight for our country, for our liberty, for our life; they contend for what but little concerns them, the power of a small party. Attack them, therefore, with so much the greater confidence, and call to mind your achievements of old.

We might, with the utmost ignominy, have passed the rest of our days in exile. Some of you, after losing your property, might have waited at

Rome for assistance from others. But because such a life, to men of spirit, was disgusting and unendurable, you resolved upon your present course. If you wish to quit it, you must exert all your resolution, for none but conquerors have exchanged war for peace. To hope for safety in flight, when you have turned away from the enemy, the arms by which the body is defended, is indeed madness. In battle, those who are most afraid are always in most danger, but courage is equivalent to a rampart.

When I contemplate you, soldiers, and when I consider your past exploits, a strong hope of victory animates me. Your spirit, your age, your valour, give me confidence—to say nothing of necessity, which makes even cowards brave. To prevent the numbers of the enemy from surrounding us, our confined situation is sufficient. But should fortune be unjust to your valour, take care not to lose your lives unavenged; take care not to be taken and butchered like cattle, rather than fighting like men, to leave to your enemies a bloody and mournful victory.

Boudicca Addresses Her Army, AD 60 or 61
From Tacitus, Annals, AD 109

Boudicca (also known as Boudica and Boadicea) was a queen of the Iceni tribe of eastern Britain who led an uprising against the invading Romans. The Roman historian Tacitus describes her rallying her troops prior to a decisive battle. Despite her exhortations, her army was slaughtered and she was killed. Her speech invokes her lost liberty, war wounds and raped daughters, and states that her cause is favoured by the gods. She ends with a dig at her male charges: 'the men, if they please, may survive with infamy, and live in bondage'.

Boudicca, in a [chariot], with her two daughters before her, drove through the ranks. She harangued the different nations in their turn. 'This', she said, 'is not the first time that the Britons have been led to battle by a woman'. But now she did not come to boast the pride of a long line of ancestry, nor even to recover her kingdom and the plundered wealth of her family. She took to the field, like the meanest among them, to assert

the cause of public liberty, and to seek revenge for her body seamed with ignominious stripes, and her two daughters infamously ravished. [She spoke as follows]:

'From the pride and arrogance of the Romans nothing is sacred; all are subject to violation; the old endure the scourge, and the virgins are deflowered. But the vindictive gods are now at hand. A Roman legion dared to face the war-like Britons: with their lives they paid for their rashness; those who survived the carnage of that day lie poorly hid behind their entrenchments, meditating nothing but how to save themselves by an ignominious flight. From the din of preparation, and the shouts of the British army, the Romans, even now, shrink back with terror. What will be their case when the assault begins? Look round, and view your numbers. Behold the proud display of war-like spirits, and consider the motives for which we draw the avenging sword. On this spot we must either conquer, or die with glory. There is no alternative. Though a woman, my resolution is fixed: the men, if they please, may survive with infamy, and live in bondage.'

FIGHTING POEM

Beowulf

Beowulf spake, and a battle-vow made
his last of all: 'I have lived through many
wars in my youth; now once again,
old folk-defender, feud will I seek,
do doughty deeds, if the dark destroyer
forth from his cavern come to fight me!'
Then hailed he the helmeted heroes all,
for the last time greeting his liegemen dear,
comrades of war: 'I should carry no weapon,
no sword to the serpent, if sure I knew
how, with such enemy, else my vows
I could gain as I did in Grendel's day.
But fire in this fight I must fear me now,
and poisonous breath; so I bring with me
breastplate and board. From the barrow's
    keeper
no footbreadth flee I. One fight shall end
our war by the wall, as Wyrd allots,
all mankind's master. My mood is bold
but forbears to boast o'er this battling-
    flyer.

>   —Now abide by the barrow, ye breastplate-mailed,
> ye heroes in harness, which of us twain
> better from battle-rush bear his wounds.
> Wait ye the finish. The fight is not yours,
> nor meet for any but me alone
> to measure might with this monster here
> and play the hero. Hardily I
> shall win that wealth, or war shall seize,
> cruel killing, your king and lord!'

This anonymous Anglo-Saxon poem dates from between the eighth and eleventh centuries, and recounts the story of the hero Beowulf, who battles a range of adversaries in his quest to keep Geat (modern-day Sweden) free from invaders, including a dragon. This excerpt takes place just before Beowulf slays the dragon. He later dies from the injuries he receives in that struggle.

'Be Ye the Avengers of Noble Blood'
William the Conqueror, Hastings, England, 1066

In 1051, William, Duke of Normandy (1028–87), visited his cousin, Edward the Confessor, King of England. He believed (or claimed) that the heirless Edward had offered him the English throne on his death, but, in 1066, Earl Harold of Wessex was crowned instead. Infuriated by this betrayal, William invaded the south of England while the English army was occupied with defeating Norse invaders in the north. On 14 October, after weeks of undisturbed looting and pillaging, William's troops faced Harold's returning army at the Battle of Hastings. Within hours Harold had been killed, his army routed and all effective resistance ended. William was crowned on Christmas Day, and by 1072 had conquered and united all of England.

William delivered this speech to his troops on the morning of the Battle of Hastings. Consisting mostly of a series of rhetorical questions, it remembers past glories, and calls for vengeance against previous English atrocities and betrayals.

Normans! bravest of nations! I have no doubt of your courage, and none of your victory, which never by any chance or obstacle escaped your efforts. If indeed you had, once only, failed to conquer, there might be a need now to inflame your courage by exhortation; but your native spirit does not require to be roused. Bravest of men, what could the power of the Frankish king effect with all his people, from Lorraine to Spain, against Hastings my predecessor? What he wanted of France he took, and gave to the king only what he pleased. What he had, he held as long as it suited him, and relinquished it only for something better. Did not Rollo my ancestor, founder of our nation, with our fathers conquer at Paris the King of the Franks in the heart of his kingdom, nor had the King of the Franks any hope of safety until he humbly offered his daughter and possession of the country, which, after you, is called Normandy.

Did not your fathers capture the King of the Franks at Rouen, and keep him there until he restored Normandy to Duke Richard, then a boy; with this condition, that, in every conference between the King of France and the Duke of

Normandy, the duke should wear his sword, while the king should not be permitted to carry a sword nor even a dagger. This concession your fathers compelled the great king to submit to, as binding for ever. Did not the same duke lead your fathers to Mirmande, at the foot of the Alps, and enforce submission from the lord of the town, his son-in-law, to his own wife, the duke's daughter? Nor was it enough for you to conquer men, he conquered the devil himself, with whom he wrestled, cast down and bound him with his hands behind his back, and left him a shameful spectacle to angels. But why do I talk of former times? Did not you, in our own time, engage the Franks at Mortemer? Did not the Franks prefer flight to battle, and use their spurs? While you—Ralph, the commander of the Franks having been slain—reaped the honour and the spoil as the natural result of your usual success. Ah! let any one of the English whom, a hundred times, our predecessors, both Danes and Normans, have defeated in battle, come forth and show that the race of Rollo ever suffered a defeat from his time until now, and I will withdraw conquered. Is it not, therefore, shameful that a people accustomed to be conquered, a people ignorant of war, a people even without arrows, should proceed in order of battle against you, my brave men? Is it not a shame that King Harold, perjured as he was in your presence, should dare to show his face to you? It is amazing to me that you have been allowed to see those who, by a horrible crime, beheaded your relations and Alfred my kinsman, and that their own heads are still on their shoulders. Raise your standards, my brave men, and set neither measure nor limit to your merited rage. May the lightning of your glory be seen and the thunders of your onset heard from east to west, and be ye the avengers of noble blood.

WAR CRIES

'Santiago y cierra, España!' (Saint James and attack, Spain!)
Used by Spanish soldiers during the Reconquista, the 700-year-long series of wars that started in AD 722 and saw Christians reclaim the Iberian Peninsula from the Arabs, and during the Spanish conquests in America. Saint James is the patron saint of Spain.

'Dex Aie!' (God help us!)
Shouted by the Norman invaders at the Battle of Hastings in 1066, and also by the British Royal Guernsey Light Infantry in the First World War

'Olicrosse!' (Holy Cross!) and 'Godamite!' (God Almighty!)
Used by Saxon officers at the Battle of Hastings, on 14 October 1066, against the Norman invaders. The foot soldiers cried: 'Ut! Ut! Ut!' (Out! Out! Out!).

'Denique caelum!' (Heaven at last!)
Latin war cry employed by European Christian soldiers during the Crusades, from the eleventh to the thirteenth centuries

Address at the Council of Clermont
Pope Urban, Clermont, France, 1095

In 1095, Byzantine emperor Alexius I Comnenus requested assistance from Christian Europeans against the Muslims who had occupied the Holy Land and were heading westwards with imperialist ambitions. In response, Pope Urban (1042–99) called an audience of French nobles and clergymen to Clermont, in central France, with the aim of inspiring them to take up arms.

Lest his listeners fail to be seized by religious zeal, Urban puts a pragmatic spin on his call to arms: Europe is small and overcrowded, while the Holy Land 'floweth with milk and honey'; Muslims are vile and heathen, and participation in a Holy War will ensure a future 'in the kingdom of heaven'. His call was successful, leading to the first of many Crusades and the conquest of Jerusalem in 1099.

Oh, race of Franks, race from across the mountains, race beloved and chosen by God ... set apart from all other nations ... by your Catholic faith and the honour which you render to the

holy church: to you our discourse is addressed, and for you our exhortations are intended. We wish you to know what a grievous cause has led us to your country, for it is the imminent peril threatening you and all the faithful which has brought us hither.

From the confines of Jerusalem and from the city of Constantinople a grievous report has gone forth and has repeatedly been brought to our ears; namely, that a race from the kingdom of the Persians, an accursed race, a race wholly alienated from God, 'a generation that set not their heart aright, and whose spirit was not steadfast with God', has violently invaded the lands of those Christians and has depopulated them by pillage and fire. They have led away a part of the captives into their own country, and a part they have killed by cruel tortures. They have either destroyed the churches of God or appropriated them for the rites of their own religion. They destroy the altars, after having defiled them with their uncleanness … The kingdom of the Greeks is now dismembered by them and has been deprived of territory so vast in extent that it could not be traversed in two months' time.

On whom, therefore, is the labour of avenging these wrongs and of recovering this territory incumbent, if not upon you—you, upon whom, above all other nations, God has conferred remarkable glory in arms, great courage, bodily activity and strength to humble the heads of those who resist you? Let the deeds of your ancestors encourage you and incite your minds to manly achievements: the glory and greatness of King Charlemagne, and of his son Louis, and of your other monarchs, who have destroyed the kingdoms of the Turks and have extended the sway of the holy church over lands previously pagan. Let the holy sepulchre of our Lord and Saviour, which is possessed by the unclean nations, especially arouse you, and the holy places which are now treated with ignominy and irreverently polluted with the filth of the unclean ...

But if you are hindered by love of children, parents or wife, remember what the Lord says in the Gospel, 'He that loveth father or mother more than me is not worthy of me'. 'Every one that hath forsaken houses, or brethren, or sisters, or father, or mother, or wife, or children, or lands, for my name's sake, shall receive an hundredfold, and shall inherit everlasting life.' Let none of your possessions retain you, nor solicitude for your family affairs. For this land which you inhabit, shut in on all sides by the seas and surrounded by the mountain peaks, is too narrow for your large population; nor does it abound in wealth; and it furnishes scarcely food enough for its cultivators. Hence it is that you murder and devour one another, that you wage war, and that very many among you perish in intestine strife.

Let hatred therefore depart from among you, let your quarrels end, let wars cease, and let all dissensions and controversies slumber. Enter upon the road to the holy sepulchre; wrest that land from the wicked race, and subject it to yourselves. That land which, as the scripture says, 'floweth with milk and honey' was given by God into the power of the children of Israel. Jerusalem is the centre of the earth; the land is fruitful above all others, like another paradise of delights. This spot the redeemer of mankind has made illustrious by his advent, has beautified by his sojourn, has consecrated by his passion, has redeemed by his death, has glorified by his burial.

This royal city, however, situated at the centre of the earth, is now held captive by the enemies of Christ and is subjected, by those who do not know God, to the worship of the heathen. She seeks, therefore, and desires to be liberated and ceases not to implore you to come to her aid. From you especially she asks succour, because, as we have already said, God has conferred upon you above all other nations great glory in arms. Accordingly, undertake this journey eagerly for the remission of your sins, with the assurance of the reward of imperishable glory in the kingdom of heaven.

FIGHTING WORDS

'When battle is joined, no noble knight thinks of anything other than breaking heads and arms.'
Bertran de Born, French baron and troubadour (c. 1140–1215)

'What is the function of knights? To guard the Church, to fight unbelievers, to venerate the priesthood, to protect the poor from injuries, to pour out their blood for their brothers ... and if need be, to lay down their lives.'
John of Salisbury (c. 1120–80), English author and diplomat, in his Policraticus *(1159)*

'Nothing is of greater importance in time of war than in knowing how to make the best use of a fair opportunity when it is offered.'
Niccolò Machiavelli (1469–1527), Florentine diplomat, philosopher and writer, in his Art of War *(1520)*

'Though I be a woman yet I have as good a courage answerable to my place as ever my father had.'
Elizabeth I of England (1533–1603), in response to Parliament, October 1566

Letter to King Henry VI of England
Joan of Arc, France, 22 March 1429

Joan of Arc (Jeanne d'Arc, c. 1412–31) was born in Domrémy, in eastern France, during the Hundred Years' War between France and England. During her childhood, her village was raided and burned several times. She declared that she had visions from God, telling her to recover her homeland from the English, and went to King Charles VII of France to tell him so. Impressed by her piety and determination, he sent her to lift the English siege at Orléans. She not only achieved this, but subsequently led the French army to a series of rapid victories.

However, Joan was subsequently seized by the Burgundians and sold to their English allies, who tried and convicted her of heresy and witchcraft. She was burned at the stake by the English on 30 May 1431, when she was just nineteen years old. In 1456, Pope Callixtus III reviewed the conviction, found her innocent and declared her a martyr. In 1909, the Catholic Church beatified her and in 1920 canonised her as a saint.

In this letter, Joan gives the English an opportunity to capitulate at Orléans, and warns of the consequences should they refuse. She speaks of government in holy terms, and switches back and forth between the first and third person, emphasising that she is both human and divine.

King of England, render account to the King of Heaven of your royal blood. Return the keys of all the good cities which you have seized to the Maid. She is sent by God to reclaim the royal blood, and is fully prepared to make peace, if you will give her satisfaction; that is, you must render justice, and pay back all that you have taken.

King of England, if you do not do these things, I am the commander of the military; and in whatever place I shall find your men in France, I will make them flee the country, whether they wish to or not; and if they will not obey, the Maid will have them all killed. She comes sent by the King of Heaven, body for body, to take you out of France, and the Maid promises and certifies to you that if you do not leave France she and her troops will raise a mighty outcry as has not been heard in France

in a thousand years. And believe that the King of Heaven has sent her so much power that you will not be able to harm her or her brave army.

To you, archers, noble companions in arms, and all people who are before Orléans, I say to you in God's name, go home to your own country; if you do not do so, beware of the Maid, and of the damages you will suffer. Do not attempt to remain, for you have no rights in France from God, the King of Heaven, and the Son of the Virgin Mary. It is Charles, the rightful heir, to whom God has given France, who will shortly enter Paris in a grand company. If you do not believe the news written of God and the Maid, then in whatever place we may find you, we will soon see who has the better right, God or you …

Duke of Bedford, who call yourself regent of France for the King of England, the Maid asks you not to make her destroy you. If you do not render her satisfaction, she and the French will perform the greatest feat ever done in the name of Christianity.

Done on the Tuesday of Holy Week. HEAR THE WORDS OF GOD AND THE MAID.

FIGHTING POEM

'Once More unto the Breach'

Once more unto the breach, dear friends,
    once more;
Or close the wall up with our English dead.
In peace there's nothing so becomes a man
As modest stillness and humility:
But when the blast of war blows in our ears,
Then imitate the action of the tiger;
Stiffen the sinews, summon up the blood,
Disguise fair nature with hard-favour'd rage;
Then lend the eye a terrible aspect;
Let pry through the portage of the head
Like the brass cannon; let the brow o'erwhelm it
As fearfully as doth a galled rock
O'erhang and jutty his confounded base,
Swill'd with the wild and wasteful ocean.
Now set the teeth and stretch the nostril wide,
Hold hard the breath and bend up every spirit
To his full height. On, on, you noblest English.
Whose blood is fet from fathers of war-proof!
Fathers that, like so many Alexanders,
Have in these parts from morn till even fought

And sheathed their swords for lack of argument:
Dishonour not your mothers; now attest
That those whom you call'd fathers did beget you.
Be copy now to men of grosser blood,
And teach them how to war. And you, good yeoman,
Whose limbs were made in England, show us here
The mettle of your pasture; let us swear
That you are worth your breeding; which I doubt not;
For there is none of you so mean and base,
That hath not noble lustre in your eyes.
I see you stand like greyhounds in the slips,
Straining upon the start. The game's afoot:
Follow your spirit, and upon this charge
Cry 'God for Harry, England, and Saint George!'

This famous speech, from Shakespeare's Henry V *(1599), Act III, Scene I, takes place during the Battle of Agincourt in 1415, during the Hundred Years' War between England and France. Henry's troops are holding the northern French city of Harfleur under siege. The 'breach' is a gap in the wall of the city. Henry encourages his troops to attack again, even if they have to 'close the wall with English dead'.*

'I Have the Heart of a King'
Elizabeth I, Tilbury Fort, Essex, England, 1588

Elizabeth I (1533–1603), daughter of Henry VIII and Anne Boleyn, and sometimes known as 'the Virgin Queen', was one of Britain's most loved monarchs. Her reign saw a decrease in sectarian violence between Catholics and Protestants, and a blossoming of literature, particularly drama.

Elizabeth's refusal to marry permitted her to shrewdly avoid taking sides in the many intrigues that confronted her, and led her suitors (and potential usurpers) to treat her with deference in the hope of gaining future favours. She refused to accept that women could be inferior to men, and gained acceptance among her subjects for her habits of spitting, swearing and enjoying a few beers.

In 1588, King Philip II of Spain, with the blessing and sponsorship of the pope, intended to invade England and put an end to the Protestant Reformation. His 130-strong fleet arrived in the English Channel on 20 July, but suffered a series of losses and defeats in skirmishes with the British navy. Faced with superior firepower and the brilliant tactics of Vice-Admiral Francis Drake, the Spanish were soon forced to retreat northwards, and many of their ships were wrecked by storms on the west coasts of Ireland and Scotland. The Spanish had lost 65 ships and about 10,000 men, the British fewer than 100 men and no ships.

This well-known speech was addressed to the English army and navy at Tilbury Fort, at the mouth of the Thames River, at the height of the hostilities. There is an element of hyperbole, in that Elizabeth was not actually about to 'take up arms', as she states; however, the inspirational quality of her words is unmistakable.

My loving people, we have been persuaded by some, that are careful of our safety, to take heed how we commit ourselves to armed multitudes, for fear of treachery; but I assure you, I do not desire to live to distrust my faithful and loving people.

Let tyrants fear; I have always so behaved myself that, under God, I have placed my chiefest strength and safeguard in the loyal hearts and good will of my subjects. And therefore I am come amongst you at this time, not as

for my recreation or sport, but being resolved, in the midst and heat of the battle, to live or die amongst you all; to lay down, for my God, and for my kingdom, and for my people, my honour and my blood, even in the dust.

I know I have but the body of a weak and feeble woman; but I have the heart of a king, and of a king of England, too; and think foul scorn that Parma or Spain, or any prince of Europe, should dare to invade the borders of my realms: to which, rather than any dishonour should grow by me, I myself will take up arms; I myself will be your general, judge and rewarder of every one of your virtues in the field.

I know already, by your forwardness, that you have deserved rewards and crowns; and we do assure you, on the word of a prince, they shall be duly paid you. In the mean my lieutenant general shall be in my stead, than whom never prince commanded a more noble and worthy subject; not doubting by your obedience to my general, by your concord in the camp, and by your valour in the field, we shall shortly have a famous victory over the enemies of my God, of my kingdom and of my people.

FAMOUS LAST WORDS

'Why are you weeping? Did you imagine that I was immortal?'
Louis XIV (1638–1715), French king, to his servants

'I only regret that I have but one life to lose for my country.'
Nathan Hale (1755–76), America's first spy, before the British executed him by hanging

'Pardon me, sir. I did not do it on purpose.'
Marie Antoinette (1744–93), wife of King Louis XVI of France, after she stepped on the executioner's foot as she approached the guillotine to be executed

'Only from the cold, my friend.'
Jean-Sylvain Bailly (1736–93), French astronomer and statesman, on being asked why he was shivering, prior to his execution during the French Revolution

'Thou wilt show my head to the people: it is worth showing.'
Georges Jacques Danton (1759–94), to his executioner, also during the French Revolution

'Give Me Liberty, or Give Me Death!'
Patrick Henry, Richmond, Virginia, United States, 23 March 1775

A determined advocate of republicanism, Patrick Henry (1736–99) was a prominent figure during the War of American Independence. He inspired popular agitation against the controversial Stamp Act, which forced British residents in America to pay taxes to England, and was elected Governor of Virginia for the periods 1776–79 and 1784–86.

Henry is perhaps best known for this speech, which he delivered in the House of Burgesses in Richmond, the Virginia colonial legislature. In it, he urges its members to take military action against the invading British forces.

Henry spoke without using any notes—at least none have been found—in a voice that became progressively louder, climaxing in a passionate crescendo with the now famous final words. After his speech, the vote was taken; his resolutions were passed by a margin of five, and Virginia entered the American Revolution.

No man thinks more highly than I do of the patriotism, as well as abilities, of the very worthy gentlemen who have just addressed the House. But different men often see the same subject in different lights; and, therefore, I hope that it will not be thought disrespectful to those gentlemen, if, entertaining as I do opinions of a character very opposite to theirs, I shall speak forth my sentiments freely and without reserve.

This is no time for ceremony. The question before the House is one of awful moment to this country. For my own part I consider it as nothing less than a question of freedom or slavery; and in proportion to the magnitude of the subject ought to be the freedom of the debate. It is only in this way that we can hope to arrive at truth, and fulfil the great responsibility which we hold to God and our country. Should I keep back my opinions at such a time, through fear of giving offence, I should consider myself as guilty of treason towards my country, and of an act of disloyalty towards the majesty of heaven, which I revere above all earthly kings.

Mr President, it is natural to man to indulge in the illusions of hope. We are apt to shut our eyes against a painful truth, and listen to the song of that siren, till she transforms us into beasts. Is this the part of wise men, engaged in a great and arduous struggle for liberty? Are we disposed to be of the number of those who, having eyes, see not, and having ears, hear not, the things which so nearly concern their temporal salvation?

For my part, whatever anguish of spirit it may cost, I am willing to know the whole truth—to know the worst and to provide for it. I have but one lamp by which my feet are guided; and that is the lamp of experience. I know of no way of judging of the future but by the past. And judging by the past, I wish to know what there has been in the conduct of the British ministry for the last ten years, to justify those hopes with which gentlemen have been pleased to solace themselves and the House?

Is it that insidious smile with which our petition has been lately received? Trust it not, sir; it will prove a snare to your feet. Suffer not yourselves to be betrayed with a kiss. Ask yourselves how this gracious reception of our petition comports with these war-like preparations which cover our waters and darken our land. Are fleets and armies necessary to a work of love and reconciliation? Have we shown ourselves so unwilling to be reconciled that force must be called in to win back our love? Let us not deceive ourselves, sir. These are the implements of war and subjugation—the last arguments to which kings resort. I ask gentlemen, sir, what means this martial array, if its purpose be not to force us to submission? Can gentlemen assign any other possible motives for it? Has Great Britain any enemy, in this quarter of the world, to call for all this accumulation of navies and armies?

No, sir, she has none. They are meant for us; they can be meant for no other. They are sent over to bind and rivet upon us those chains which the British ministry have been so long forging. And what have we to oppose to them? Shall we try argument? Sir, we have been trying that for the last ten years. Have we anything new to offer on the subject? Nothing.

We have held the subject up in every light of which it is capable; but it has been all in vain. Shall we resort to entreaty and humble supplication? What terms shall we find which have not been already exhausted? Let us not, I beseech you, sir, deceive ourselves longer.

Sir, we have done everything that could be done to avert the storm which is now coming on. We have petitioned; we have remonstrated; we have supplicated; we have prostrated ourselves before the throne, and have implored its interposition to arrest the tyrannical hands of the ministry and Parliament.

Our petitions have been slighted; our remonstrances have produced additional violence and insult; our supplications have been disregarded; and we have been spurned, with contempt, from the foot of the throne. In vain, after these things, may we indulge the fond hope of peace and reconciliation. There is no longer any room for hope.

If we wish to be free—if we mean to preserve inviolate those inestimable privileges for which we have been so long contending—if we mean not basely to abandon the noble struggle in which we have been so long engaged, and which we have pledged ourselves never to abandon until the glorious object of our contest shall be obtained, we must fight! I repeat it, sir, we must fight! An appeal to arms and to the God of Hosts is all that is left us!

They tell us, sir, that we are weak—unable to cope with so formidable an adversary. But when shall we be stronger? Will it be the next week, or the next year? Will it be when we are totally disarmed, and when a British guard shall be stationed in every house? Shall we gather strength by irresolution and inaction? Shall we acquire the means of effectual resistance, by lying supinely on our backs, and hugging the delusive phantom of hope, until our enemies shall have bound us hand and foot?

Sir, we are not weak, if we make a proper use of the means which the God of nature hath placed in our power. Three millions of people, armed in the holy cause of liberty, and in such a country as that which we possess, are invincible by any force which our enemy can send against us. Besides, sir, we shall not fight our battles alone. There is a just God who presides over the destinies of nations, and who will raise up friends to fight our battles for us.

The battle, sir, is not to the strong alone; it is to the vigilant, the active, the brave. Besides, sir, we have no election. If we were base enough to desire it, it is now too late to retire from the contest. There is no retreat but in submission and slavery! Our chains are forged! Their clanking may be heard on the plains of Boston! The war is inevitable—and let it come! I repeat it, sir, let it come!

It is in vain, sir, to extenuate the matter. Gentlemen may cry, 'Peace! Peace!'—but there is no peace. The war is actually begun! The next gale that sweeps from the north will bring to our ears the clash of resounding arms! Our brethren are already in the field! Why stand we here idle? What is it that gentlemen wish? What would they have? Is life so dear, or peace so sweet, as to be purchased at the price of chains and slavery? Forbid it, Almighty God! I know not what course others may take; but as for me, give me liberty, or give me death!

'We Must Dare, Dare Again, Always Dare'

Georges Jacques Danton, Paris, 2 September 1792

Parisian lawyer Georges Jacques Danton (1759–94) was a major figure in the initial stages of the French Revolution. When he made this speech to the National Assembly, France was being attacked by Austrian and Prussian armies, which, contrary to Danton's assertion, had already captured Verdun.

Danton became Minister of Justice and the predominant member of the Executive Committee. But after two years of massacres, which he did little to prevent, the voters dumped him. He was guillotined on 5 April 1794 for antirevolutionary activity.

It is gratifying to the ministers of a free people to have to announce to them that their country will be saved. All are stirred, all are excited, all burn to fight. You know that Verdun is not yet in the power of our enemies. You know that its garrison swears to immolate the first who breathes a proposition of surrender.

One portion of our people will proceed to the frontiers, another will throw up entrenchments, and the third with pikes will defend the hearts of our cities. Paris will second these great efforts. The commissioners of the Commune will solemnly proclaim to the citizens the invitation to arm and march to the defence of the country. At such a moment you can proclaim that the capital deserves well of all France.

At such a moment this National Assembly becomes a veritable committee of war. We ask that you concur with us in directing this sublime movement of the people, by naming commissioners who will second us in these great measures. We ask that any one refusing to give personal service or to furnish arms shall be punished with death. We ask that a set of instructions be drawn up for the citizens to direct their movements. We ask that couriers be sent to all the departments to notify them of the decrees that you proclaim here. The tocsin we are about to ring is not an alarm signal; it sounds the charge on the enemies of our country. To conquer them we must dare, dare again, always dare, and France is saved!

FIGHTING SONG

La Marseillaise

Allons enfants de la Patrie,
Le jour de gloire est arrivé !
Contre nous de la tyrannie,
L'étendard sanglant est levé,
L'étendard sanglant est levé,
Entendez-vous, dans les campagnes
Mugir ces féroces soldats ?
Ils viennent jusque dans vos bras
Égorger vos fils, vos compagnes !

Aux armes, citoyens,
Formez vos bataillons,
Marchons, marchons !
Qu'un sang impur
Abreuve nos sillons !

Let us go, children of the fatherland
Our day of Glory has arrived.
Against us stands tyranny,
The bloody flag is raised,
The bloody flag is raised.
Do you hear in the countryside
The roar of these savage soldiers
They come right into your arms
To cut the throats of your sons, your country.

To arms, citizens!
Form your battalions!
Let us march, let us march!
That their impure blood
Should water our fields!

'La Marseillaise', the national anthem of France, was written in April 1792 (at the height of the French Revolution) by Claude Joseph Rouget de Lisle, and was originally called the 'War Song for the Army of the Rhine'. After being taken up by volunteer soldiers from Marseille (hence the song's name), it became a rallying call for revolutionaries and was officially adopted as the national anthem on 14 July 1795.

Farewell to the Old Guard
Napoleon Bonaparte, Paris, 20 April 1814

A general in the French Revolution of 1789–99, Napoleon (1769–1821) seized power in 1799 and crowned himself Emperor of France in 1804. By 1808, he had conquered much of Europe and agreed to divide the continent with Russia. But when the Russians refused to cooperate in France's blockade of Britain in 1812, Napoleon invaded Russia. He seriously underestimated that nation's strength and the severity of its winter, and his army was routed by a coalition of Austria, Russia, Prussia, Sweden and the United Kingdom.

Forced to abdicate, Napoleon was banished to the island of Elba in 1814. But he managed to escape in February 1815, returning to France, where he cobbled together an 'Old Guard' army of still-loyal soldiers. He regained power for about one hundred days, but was again forced to abdicate following his defeat at the Battle of Waterloo in June 1815. He was then exiled to the island of St Helena, in the South Atlantic Ocean, where he died in 1821.

In this speech, made at Fontainebleau after his first abdication, Napoleon bids farewell to the officers of the Old Guard, who presumably believed his ridiculous, conceited claim, 'I have sacrificed all of my interests to those of the country'.

Soldiers of my Old Guard: I bid you farewell. For twenty years I have constantly accompanied you on the road to honour and glory. In these latter times, as in the days of our prosperity, you have invariably been models of courage and fidelity. With men such as you our cause could not be lost; but the war would have been interminable; it would have been civil war, and that would have entailed deeper misfortunes on France.

I have sacrificed all of my interests to those of the country.

I go, but you, my friends, will continue to serve France. Her happiness was my only thought. It will still be the object of my wishes. Do not regret my fate; if I have consented to survive, it is to serve your glory. I intend to write the history of the great achievements we have performed together. Adieu, my friends. Would I could press you all to my heart.

NAPOLEON BONAPARTE

General and emperor, Napoleon Bonaparte was responsible for numerous bon mots, including:

'An army marches on its stomach.'

'A great people may be killed, but they cannot be intimidated.'

'Soldiers: Behold your colours! These eagles will always be your rallying point! They will always be where your emperor may think them necessary for the defence of his throne and of his people. Swear to sacrifice your lives to defend them, and by your courage to keep them constantly in the path of victory. Swear!'
Address to troops, 3 December 1804

'Soldiers: This is the battle you have so much desired. The victory depends upon you! ... Let the latest posterity recount with pride your conduct on this day; let them say of you, "He was at the battle under the walls of Moscow".'
Speech before the Battle of Borodino, 7 September 1812

'To Arms, All—All of You!'
Giuseppe Garibaldi, Naples, Italy, 1860

Italian patriot and military commander Giuseppe Garibaldi (1807–82) helped end the occupation of Italy by Britain, France, Austria and other vested interests. In 1860, he took Sicily from the British, then moved north, gathering 'red-shirt' volunteers as he won a series of victories. In August 1860, he took Naples; a year later, Italy's independence was proclaimed. This speech to his soldiers was made in Naples prior to the successful campaign.

… Yes, young men … You have conquered and you will conquer still, because you are prepared for the tactics that decide the fate of battles. You are not unworthy of the men who entered the ranks of a Macedonian phalanx, and who contended not in vain with the proud conquerors of Asia. To this wonderful page in our country's history another more glorious still will be added, and the slave shall show at last to his free brothers a sharpened sword forged from the links of his fetters.

To arms, then, all of you! all of you! And the oppressors and the mighty shall disappear like dust. You, too, women, cast away all the cowards from your embraces; they will give you only cowards for children, and you who are the daughters of the land of beauty must bear children who are noble and brave. Let timid doctrinaires depart from among us to carry their servility and their miserable fears elsewhere. This people is its own master. It wishes to be the brother of other peoples, but to look on the insolent with a proud glance, not to grovel before them imploring its own freedom. It will no longer follow in the trail of men whose hearts are foul. No! No! No!

Providence has presented Italy with Victor Emmanuel. Every Italian should rally round him. By the side of Victor Emmanuel every quarrel should be forgotten, all rancour depart. Once more I repeat my battle cry: 'To arms, all—all of you!' If March, 1861, does not find one million of Italians in arms, then alas for liberty, alas for the life of Italy. Ah, no, far be from me a thought which I loathe like poison. March of 1861, or if need be February, will find us all at our post—Italians of Calatafimi,

Palermo, Ancona, the Volturno, Castelfidardo and Isernia, and with us every man of this land who is not a coward or a slave. Let all of us rally round the glorious hero of Palestro and give the last blow to the crumbling edifice of tyranny. Receive, then, my gallant young volunteers, at the honoured conclusion of ten battles, one word of farewell from me.

I utter this word with deepest affection and from the very bottom of my heart. Today I am obliged to retire, but for a few days only. The hour of battle will find me with you again, by the side of the champions of Italian liberty. Let those only return to their homes who are called by the imperative duties which they owe to their families, and those who by their glorious wounds have deserved the credit of their country. These, indeed, will serve Italy in their homes by their counsel, by the very aspect of the scars which adorn their youthful brows. Apart from these, let all others remain to guard our glorious banners. We shall meet again before long to march together to the redemption of our brothers who are still slaves of the stranger. We shall meet again before long to march to new triumphs.

Gettysburg Address
Abraham Lincoln, Gettysburg, Pennsylvania, United States, 19 November 1863

The election of Abraham Lincoln (1809–65) as US president in 1860, largely on an antislavery ticket, triggered the US Civil War, which broke out in April 1861. After 600,000 were killed, the war ended in April 1865 with victory to Lincoln and the North. The result was the abolition of slavery, and the reunification of North and South.

Lincoln made this speech as he dedicated a military cemetery at Gettysburg, Pennsylvania. 'Four score and seven years ago' refers to the War of American Independence (1775–83). Lincoln discusses the Civil War as part of a wider struggle to protect the principles of democracy and freedom.

Four score and seven years ago our fathers brought forth on this continent a new nation, conceived in Liberty, and dedicated to the proposition that all men are created equal.

Now we are engaged in a great civil war, testing whether that nation, or any nation so

conceived and so dedicated, can long endure. We are met on a great battlefield of that war. We have come to dedicate a portion of that field, as a final resting place for those who here gave their lives that that nation might live. It is altogether fitting and proper that we should do this.

But, in a larger sense, we cannot dedicate, we cannot consecrate, we cannot hallow this ground. The brave men, living and dead, who struggled here, have consecrated it, far above our poor power to add or detract. The world will little note, nor long remember what we say here, but it can never forget what they did here. It is for us the living, rather, to be dedicated here to the unfinished work which they who fought here have thus far so nobly advanced. It is rather for us to be here dedicated to the great task remaining before us, that from these honoured dead we take increased devotion to that cause for which they gave the last full measure of devotion, that we here highly resolve that these dead shall not have died in vain, that this nation, under God, shall have a new birth of freedom, and that government of the people, by the people, for the people, shall not perish from the earth.

FIGHTING WORDS

'A diplomat who says "yes" means "maybe"; a diplomat who says "maybe" means "no" and a diplomat who says "no" is no diplomat.'
Charles de Talleyrand (1754–1838), French envoy under Napoleon

'It is well that war is so terrible. We should grow too fond of it.'
Robert E. Lee (1807–70), Confederate general in the American Civil War

'There is many a boy here today who looks on war as all glory, but, boys, it is all hell.'
William T. Sherman (1820–91), educator, author and soldier, and a brilliant Union general in the American Civil War. This famous quote was made during an address to the graduating class of the Michigan Military Academy on 19 June 1879.

'As soon as war is looked upon as wicked, it will always have its fascination. When it is looked upon as vulgar, it will cease to be popular.'
Oscar Wilde (1854–1900), Irish writer

Last Speech
Abraham Lincoln, Washington, D.C., 11 April 1865

Two days after the surrender of Confederate general Robert E. Lee's army, and with the end of the US Civil War imminent, Lincoln delivered this speech in front of a jubilant crowd outside the White House. Lincoln appeared at the window over the building's main door.

For the first time in public, Lincoln expressed his support of black suffrage, which so enraged John Wilkes Booth, a white supremacist in the audience, that he vowed, 'That is the last speech he will make'. Three days later, Booth shot Lincoln from behind while the president and his wife were watching the farce *Our American Cousin* at Ford's Theater in New York. Eight people were convicted of conspiring in the assassination. Four were hanged, including Mary Surratt, the first woman to be executed by the US government.

Lincoln's speech is remarkably free of triumphalism; rather it suggests ways to reconstruct the war-ravaged country and redress past injustices.

… By these recent successes the reinauguration of the national authority—reconstruction—which has had a large share of thought from the first, is pressed much more closely upon our attention. It is fraught with great difficulty. Unlike the case of a war between independent nations, there is no authorised organ for us to treat with. No one man has authority to give up the rebellion for any other man. We simply must begin with, and mould from, disorganised and discordant elements. Nor is it a small additional embarrassment that we, the loyal people, differ among ourselves as to the mode, manner, and means of reconstruction. As a general rule, I abstain from reading the reports of attacks upon myself, wishing not to be provoked by that to which I cannot properly offer an answer. In spite of this precaution, however, it comes to my knowledge that I am much censured for some supposed agency in setting up, and seeking to sustain, the new state government of Louisiana. In this I have done just so much as, and no more than, the public knows. In the Annual Message of December 1863 and accompanying proclamation, I presented a plan of reconstruction (as the phrase goes) which, I promised, if adopted by any state, should be acceptable to, and sustained by, the executive government of the nation. I distinctly stated that this was not the only plan which might possibly be acceptable; and I also distinctly protested that the executive claimed no right to say when, or whether members should be admitted to seats in Congress from such states. This plan was, in advance, submitted to the then cabinet, and distinctly approved by every member of it ...

The message went to Congress, and I received many commendations of the plan, written and verbal; and not a single objection to it, from any professed emancipationist, came to my knowledge, until after the news reached Washington that the people of Louisiana had begun to move in accordance with it ...

I have been shown a letter on this subject, supposed to be an able one, in which the writer expresses regret that my mind has not seemed to be definitely fixed on the question whether the seceded states, so called, are in the Union or out of it. It would perhaps add astonishment to his regret, were he to learn that since I have found professed Union men endeavouring to make that question, I have purposely forborne any public expression upon it. As appears to me that question has not been, nor yet is, a practically material one, and that any discussion of it, while it thus remains practically immaterial, could have no effect other than the mischievous one of dividing our friends. As yet, whatever it may hereafter become, that question is bad, as the basis of a controversy, and good for nothing at all—a merely pernicious abstraction.

We all agree that the seceded states, so called, are out of their proper practical relation with the Union; and that the sole object of the government, civil and military, in regard to those states is to again get them into that proper practical relation. I believe it is not only possible, but in fact, easier, to do this, without deciding, or even considering, whether these states have ever been out of the Union, than with it. Finding themselves safely at home, it would be utterly immaterial whether they had ever been abroad. Let us all join in doing the acts necessary to restoring the proper practical relations between these states and the Union; and each forever after, innocently indulge his own opinion whether, in doing the acts, he brought the states from without, into the Union, or only gave them proper assistance, they never having been out of it ...

Some 12,000 voters in the heretofore slave-state of Louisiana have sworn allegiance to the Union, assumed to be the rightful political power of the state, held elections, organised a state government, adopted a free-state constitution, giving the benefit of public schools equally to black and white, and empowering the legislature to confer the elective franchise upon the coloured man. Their legislature has already voted to ratify the constitutional amendment recently passed by Congress, abolishing slavery throughout the nation. These 12,000 persons are thus fully committed to the Union, and to perpetual freedom in the state—committed to the very things, and nearly all the things the nation wants—and they ask the nation's recognition, and its assistance to make good their committal. Now, if we reject and spurn them, we do our utmost to disorganise and disperse them. We in effect say to the white men 'You are worthless, or worse—we will neither help you, nor be helped by you'. To the blacks we say 'This cup of liberty which these, your old masters, hold to your lips, we will dash from you, and leave you to the chances of gathering the spilled and scattered contents in some vague and undefined when, where and how'. If this course, discouraging and paralysing both white and black, has any tendency to bring Louisiana into proper practical relations with the Union, I have, so far, been unable to perceive it. If, on the contrary, we recognise and sustain the new government of Louisiana the converse of all this is made true. We encourage the hearts, and nerve the arms of the 12,000 to adhere to their work, and argue for it, and proselyte for it, and fight for it, and feed it, and grow it, and ripen it to a complete success. The coloured man too, in seeing all united for him, is inspired with vigilance, and energy, and daring, to the same end. Grant that he desires the elective franchise, will he not attain it sooner by saving the already advanced steps toward it, than by running backward over them?

'I Will Fight No More Forever'
Chief Joseph, Montana, United States, 5 October 1877

Joseph, also known as 'Thunder Travelling to the Loftier Mountain Heights' (1840–1904), was chief of the Nez Perce Native American tribe of northwestern Oregon. After a series of negotiations, in 1877 the tribe was ordered by the invading US army to relocate to a reservation. Chief Joseph agreed, but some young men of the tribe killed four white men—an act of war. In an attempt to escape to freedom in Canada, Joseph led about 800 of his people across Oregon, Washington, Idaho, Wyoming and Montana. On the way, they battled some 2000 US army troops, impressing US General Oliver O. Howard with their effective use of advance and rear guards, pincer and diversionary tactics, and field fortifications.

After a journey of more than 1600 kilometres (1000 miles), the remaining 431 Nez Perce were finally trapped just 64 kilometres (40 miles) from the Canadian border. At the end of a five-day battle in the Bear Paw Mountains, Montana, in freezing conditions and having no food or blankets, Joseph formally surrendered. This is the speech he made.

Tell General Howard I know his heart. What he told me before, I have it in my heart. I am tired of fighting. Our chiefs are killed; Looking Glass is dead, Ta-Hul-Hul-Shote is dead. The old men are all dead. It is the young men who say yes or no. He who led on the young men is dead. It is cold, and we have no blankets; the little children are freezing to death. My people, some of them, have run away to the hills, and have no blankets, no food. No one knows where they are—perhaps freezing to death. I want to have time to look for my children, and see how many of them I can find. Maybe I shall find them among the dead. Hear me, my chiefs! I am tired; my heart is sick and sad. From where the sun now stands, I will fight no more forever.

FIGHTING SONG

The Star-Spangled Banner

O! say can you see by the dawn's early light
What so proudly we hailed at the twilight's last
    gleaming?
Whose broad stripes and bright stars through the
    perilous fight,
O'er the ramparts we watched were so gallantly
    streaming?
And the rockets' red glare, the bombs bursting in air,
Gave proof through the night that our flag was still there.
O! say does that star-spangled banner yet wave
O'er the land of the free and the home of the brave?

On the shore, dimly seen through the mists of the
    deep,
Where the foe's haughty host in dread silence reposes,
What is that which the breeze, o'er the towering steep,
As it fitfully blows, half conceals, half discloses?
Now it catches the gleam of the morning's first beam,
In full glory reflected now shines in the stream:
'Tis the star-spangled banner! Oh long may it wave
O'er the land of the free and the home of the brave.

And where is that band who so vauntingly swore,
That the havoc of war and the battle's confusion,
A home and a country should leave us no more?
Their blood has washed out their foul footsteps' pollution;
No refuge could save the hireling and slave
From the terror of flight, or the gloom of the grave:
And the star-spangled banner in triumph doth wave
O'er the land of the free and the home of the brave!

Oh! thus be it ever, when freemen shall stand
Between their loved home and the war's desolation!
Blessed with victory and peace, may the heav'n-rescued land
Praise the Power that hath made and preserved us a nation.
Then conquer we must, when our cause it is just,
And this be our motto, 'In God is our trust'.
And the star-spangled banner in triumph shall wave
O'er the land of the free and the home of the brave!

This song has been the US national anthem since 3 March 1931. The words, from an 1814 poem by Francis Scott Key (1779–1843), were set to the tune of a popular British drinking song.

The 'Four Minute Men'
Volunteer speeches, United States, 1917–18

During the First World War, American president Woodrow Wilson set up the Committee on Public Information (CPI)—headed by journalist George Creel and, consequently, also known as the Creel Committee—to control the release of news and solicit public support for the war. The CPI produced a flood of propaganda and also organised the 'Four Minute Men', an army of volunteers who gave brief prowar speeches in public places, notably movie theatres—they were so named because they often gave their speeches in the four minutes it took to change movie reels. Creel later claimed that 75,000 orators delivered 7.5 million speeches to more than 314 million people. Reprinted here are some of his suggestions for delivering a brief, effective 'sound bite', and a selection of the speeches.

General Suggestions to Speakers

The speech must not be longer than four minutes, which means there is no time for a single

wasted word. Speakers should go over their speech time and time again until the ideas are firmly fixed in their mind and cannot be forgotten. This does not mean that the speech needs to be written out and committed (memorised), although most speakers, especially when limited in time, do best to commit.

Divide your speech carefully into certain divisions, say 15 seconds for final appeal; 45 seconds to describe the bond; 15 seconds for opening words, etc, etc. Any plan is better than none, and it can be amended every day in the light of experience.

There never was a speech yet that couldn't be improved. Never be satisfied with success. Aim to be more successful, and still more successful. So keep your eyes open. Read all the papers every day, to find a new slogan, or a new phraseology, or a new idea to replace something you have in your speech. For instance, the editorial page of the *Chicago Herald* of May 19 is crammed full of good ideas and phrases. Most of the article is a little above the average audience, but if the ideas are good, you should plan carefully to bring them into the experience of your auditors. There is one sentence which says, 'No country was ever saved by the other fellow; it must be done by you, by a hundred million yous, or it will not be done at all'. Or again, Secretary [William] McAdoo says, 'Every dollar invested in the Liberty Loan is a real blow for liberty, a blow against the militaristic system which would strangle the freedom of the world', and so on. Both the *Tribune* and the *Examiner*, besides the *Herald*, contain President Wilson's address to the nation in connection with the draft registration. The latter part is very suggestive and can be used effectively. Try slogans like 'Earn the right to say, I helped to win the war', and 'This is a Loyalty Bond as well as a Liberty Bond', or 'A cause that is worth living for is worth dying for, and a cause that is worth dying for is worth fighting for'. Conceive of your speech as a mosaic made up of five or six hundred words, each one of which has its function.

Get your friends to criticise you pitilessly. We all want to do our best and naturally like to be praised, but there is nothing so dangerous as 'josh' and 'jolly'. Let your friends know that you want ruthless criticism. If their criticism isn't sound, you can reject it. If it is sound, wouldn't you be foolish to reject it?

Be sure to prepare very carefully your closing appeal, whatever it may be, so that you may not leave your speech hanging in the air.

Don't yield to the inspiration of the moment, or to applause to depart from your speech outline. This does not mean that you may not add a word or two, but remember that one can speak only 130, or 140, or 150 words a minute, and if your speech has been carefully prepared to fill four minutes, you cannot add anything to your speech without taking away something of serious importance.

Cut out 'Doing your bit'. 'Business as usual.' 'Your country needs you.' They are flat and no longer have any force or meaning.

Time yourself in advance on every paragraph and remember you are likely to speak somewhat more slowly in public than when you practise in your own room.

There are several good ideas and statements in the printed speech recently sent you. Look it up at once.

If you come across a new slogan, or a new argument, or a new story, or a new illustration, don't fail to send it to the Committee. We need your help to make the Four Minute Men the mightiest force for arousing patriotism in the United States.

I Am

I am the man who speaks throughout the length and breadth of our country.

I look east out past the Statue of Liberty towards the flaming battle line.

The sun sets in the Pacific as I work along our western shores.

The Southland hears my call, Canada knows I am her friend.

I am in the War Department, the Treasury, the cantonments, factories and shipyards, in the busy city office, and in the country store beside the cracker barrel.

I am on active duty every evening.

I see the city's dazzling lights and the country's twinkling lamps.

I am poor and rich, young and old.

I build morale and confidence in the right.

I defeat fear, mistrust and ignorance.

Lies are cut down and fall naked before my sword.

False rumour flies before the searchlight of my truth as does the mist at sunrise.

I make clear the issues so that all may know and understand.

It is my duty 'to hold unbroken the inner lines', [and] 'to inspire to highest action and noblest sacrifice'.

I am everywhere helping to win this greatest of wars and to save the world for God and man.

I am here to stay on duty until the fight is won.

I am the Four Minute Man.

It's Duty Boy

My boy must never bring disgrace to his
    immortal sires—
At Valley Forge and Lexington they kindled
    freedom's fires,
John's father died at Gettysburg, mine fell at
    Chancellorsville;
While John himself was with the boys who
    charged up San Juan Hill.
And John, if he was living now, would surely say
    with me,
'No son of ours shall e'er disgrace our grand old
    family tree

By turning out a slacker when his country needs his aid'.
It is not of such timber that America was made.
I'd rather you had died at birth or not been born at all,
Than know that I had raised a son who cannot hear the call
That freedom has sent round the world, its previous rights to save—
This call is meant for you, my boy, and I would have you brave;
And though my heart is breaking, boy, I bid you do your part,
And show the world no son of mine is cursed with craven heart;
And if, perchance, you ne'er return, my later days to cheer,
And I have only memories of my brave boy, so dear,
I'd rather have it so, my boy, and know you bravely died
Than have a living coward sit supinely by my side.
To save the world from sin, my boy, God gave his only son—
He's asking for My boy, today, and may His will be done.

Against Conscription & War
Emma Goldman, New York, 14 June 1917

Widely known as 'Red Emma', Emma Goldman (1869–1940) was a Lithuanian-born anarchist who migrated to the United States with her family in 1886. Working in the textile industry, she became outraged by the working and social conditions in what she had expected to be a land of opportunity and freedom. She became an activist for women's rights, anticonscription and the violent overthrow of the government. She was arrested and jailed several times, then deported to the USSR in 1919, but returned to the United States in 1924. She published an autobiography, *Living My Life* (1931), and several anarchist works.

She made this speech in New York at a meeting of the No-Conscription League, ten weeks after the US entered the First World War. Shortly afterwards she was fined US$10,000 and jailed for two years for opposing conscription. Goldman, who had received a death threat warning her not to attend the meeting, was introduced, to wild applause, by the chairman as having 'more courage than half a dozen regiments'.

This is not the place to applaud or shout Hurrah for Emma Goldman. We have more serious things to talk about and some serious things to do …

Friends, tomorrow morning I am sure that you will read the report that a meeting took place on the East Side attended by foreigners, by workmen, and ill-kempt, poorly washed people of the East Side—foreigners who are being jeered at the present time in this country, foreigners who are being ridiculed because they have an idea. Well, friends, if the Americans are to wait until Americans wake up the country, they will have to resurrect the Indians who were killed in America and upon whose bodies this so-called democracy was established, because every other American, if you scratch him, you will find him to be an Englishman, Dutchman, Frenchman, Spaniard, a Jew and a German and a hundred and one other nationalities who sent their young men and their women to this country in the foolish belief that liberty was awaiting them at the American Harbour, Liberty holding a torch. That torch has been burning dimly in the United States for a very long time. It is because the

Goddess of Liberty is ashamed of the American people and what they have done in the name of liberty to liberty in the United States ...

Evidently, America has to learn a salutary lesson and it is going to pay a terrible price. It is going to shed oceans of blood, it is going to heap mountains of human sacrifices of men of this country who are able to create and produce, to whom the future belongs. They are to be slaughtered in blood and in sacrifice in the name of a thing which has never yet existed in the United States of America, in the name of democracy and liberty ...

The people were never asked whether they wanted war. Indeed, the people of America placed Mr Wilson in the White House and in the Chair of the Presidency because he told the people that he would keep them out of war, and as one of his political advertisements billposters were posted all over the city with the picture of a working woman and her children saying, 'He has kept us out of war'. He promised you heaven, he promised you everything if you would only place him in power. What made you place him in power. You expected peace and not war. The moment you placed him in power, however, he forgot his promises and he is giving you hell. War was imposed upon the people without the people getting a chance to say whether they wanted war or not, and war was imposed upon them, I say, because the gentlemen of power and those who back power want war ...

I deny that the President or those who back the President have any right to tell the people that they shall take their sons and husbands and brothers and lovers and shall conscript them in order to ship them across the seas for the conquest of militarism and the support of wealth and power in the United States. You say that is a law. I deny your law. I don't believe in it.

The only law that I recognise is the law which ministers to the needs of humanity, which makes men and women finer and better and more humane, the kind of law which teaches children that human life is sacred, and that those who arm for the purpose of taking human life are going to be called before the bar of human justice and not before a wretched little court which is called your law of the United States. And so, friends, the people have not yet decided whether they want war and the people are going to say, ultimately, whether they want war or not ...

If the framers of the Declaration of Independence, if Jefferson or Henry or the others, if they could look down upon the country and see what their offspring has done to it, how they have outraged it, how they have robbed it, how they have polluted it—why, my friends, they would turn in their graves. They would rise again and they would cleanse this country from its internal enemies, and that is the ruling class of the United States. There is a lesson you are going to learn and terrible as it is for us we nevertheless are glad that you will have to learn that lesson ...

To threaten anyone's life, to say that she will not come back from a meeting alive—how stupid. What is life unless you can live it in freedom and in beauty, and unless you can express yourself, unless you can be true to yourself what is life? I would rather than live the life of a dog to be compelled to sneak about and slink about, to worry that somebody is looking for you ready to take your life—Rather than that I would die the death of a lion any day ...

Nothing but the human mind, nothing but human emotions, nothing but an intense passion for a great ideal, nothing but perseverance and devotion and strength of character—nothing else ever solved any problem ...

I wish to say here, and I don't say it with any authority and I don't say it as a prophet, I merely tell you—I merely tell you the more people you lock up, the more will be the idealists who will take their place; the more of the human voice you suppress, the greater and louder and the profounder will be the human voice. At present it is a mere rumbling, but that rumbling is increasing in volume, it is growing in depth, it is spreading all over the country until it will be raised into a thunder and people of America will rise and say, we want to be a democracy, to be sure, but we want the kind of democracy which means liberty and opportunity to every man and woman in America.

FIGHTING WORDS

'War is a series of catastrophes that results in a victory.'
Georges Clemenceau (1841–1929), prime minister of France, 1919

'You will be home before the leaves have fallen from the trees.'
Kaiser Wilhelm II (1859–1941), German head of state, addressing his troops in August 1914

'I realise that patriotism is not enough. I must have no hatred or bitterness towards anyone.'
Edith Cavell (1865–1915), British nurse. She was executed by the Germans for helping Allied soldiers, on 11 October 1915, the day after making this statement.

'Enormous masses of ammunition, such as the human mind had never imagined before the war, were hurled upon the bodies of men who passed a miserable existence scattered about in mud-filled shell-holes ... It was no longer life at all. It was mere unspeakable suffering.'
Erich von Ludendorff (1865–1937), German general, 1920

'Germany Expected to Find a Lamb & Found a Lion'
David Lloyd George, London, 21 June 1917

In this speech to the British Parliament, David Lloyd George (1863–1945), prime minister from 1916 to 1922, refutes the idea that Britain was responsible for the outbreak of the First World War, and ridicules the Germans' propaganda efforts to paint England, specifically, as the aggressor.

It is a satisfaction for Britain in these terrible times that no share of the responsibility for these events rests on her.

She is not the Jonah in this storm. The part taken by our country in this conflict, in its origin, and in its conduct, has been as honourable and chivalrous as any part ever taken in any country in any operation.

We might imagine from declarations which were made by the Germans, aye! and even by a few people in this country, who are constantly referring to our German comrades, that this terrible war was wantonly and wickedly provoked by England—never Scotland—never Wales—and never Ireland.

Wantonly provoked by England to increase her possessions, and to destroy the influence, the power, and the prosperity of a dangerous rival.

There never was a more foolish travesty of the actual facts. It happened three years ago, or less, but there have been so many bewildering events crowded into those intervening years that some people might have forgotten, perhaps, some of the essential facts, and it is essential that we should now and again restate them, not merely to refute the calumniators of our native land, but in order to sustain the hearts of her people by the unswerving conviction that no part of the guilt of this terrible bloodshed rests on the conscience of their native land.

What are the main facts? There were six countries which entered the war at the beginning. Britain was last, and not the first.

Before she entered the war Britain made every effort to avoid it; begged, supplicated and entreated that there should be no conflict.

I was a member of the Cabinet at the time, and I remember the earnest endeavours we made to persuade Germany and Austria not to precipitate Europe into this welter of blood. We begged them to summon a European conference to consider.

Had that conference met arguments against provoking such a catastrophe that were so overwhelming there would never have been a war. Germany knew that, so she rejected the conference, although Austria was prepared to accept it. She suddenly declared war, and yet we are the people who wantonly provoked this war, in order to attack Germany.

We begged Germany not to attack Belgium, and produced a treaty, signed by the King of Prussia, as well as the King of England, pledging himself to protect Belgium against an invader, and we said, 'If you invade Belgium we shall have no alternative but to defend it'.

The enemy invaded Belgium, and now they say, 'Why, forsooth, you, England, provoked this war'.

It is not quite the story of the wolf and the lamb. I will tell you why—because Germany expected to find a lamb and found a lion.

VLADIMIR LENIN

Russian revolutionary and political leader Vladimir Ilyich Lenin (1870–1924) headed the October 1917 Revolution and became the first leader of the Soviet republic. He signed a treaty with Germany in March 1918, extracting Russia from the First World War.

'While the state exists, there can be no freedom. When there is freedom there will be no state.'
From State and Revolution, *1919*

'Communism is Soviet government plus the electrification of the whole country.'
From New External and Internal Position and the Problems of the Party, *1920*

'Germany wants revenge, and we want revolution. For the moment our aims are the same. When our ways part they will be our most ferocious and our greatest enemies. Time will tell whether a German hegemony or a Communist federation is to arise out of the ruins of Europe.'
From a prophetic speech to his followers, 1920

Speech to the Industry Club
Adolf Hitler, Dusseldorf, Germany, 27 January 1932

In early 1932, Adolf Hitler (1889–1945), leader of the German Nazi party, was planning an electoral campaign to wrest power from German president Paul von Hindenburg. But finances were a problem; as the campaign organiser and propaganda guru Dr Joseph Goebbels said: 'Money is wanting everywhere … Once you get the power you can get cash galore, but then you need it no longer. Without the power you need the money, but then you can't get it'.

The Industry Club was an agglomeration of German leaders of industry, naturally conservative and hence sceptical about Hitler's radical agenda. But in this brilliant speech, Hitler paints himself as an economic conservative who believes that foreign policy plays too great a part in German life, and at the expense of industry, productivity and profit. He dwells on the evils of communism (the communist party, like the Nazis, had recently been making large electoral gains) and the power of trade unions to stifle industry at the expense of the nation's prosperity. He mentions only two valid possible forms of government: democracy, whose outcome must be decay and mediocrity—'the rule of stupidity, of mediocrity, of half-heartedness, of cowardice, of weakness, and of inadequacy'—and authoritarianism, 'because whatever man in the past has achieved—all human civilisations—is conceivable only if the supremacy of this principle is admitted'. He quotes leaders and philosophers (selectively and out of context), his underlying message being that war is a natural and just response to exploitation by external forces, as measured by their detrimental (and obvious) effects on German industry.

The audience, cool and reserved at first, was soon eating out of Hitler's hand. His two-and-a-half-hour oration was received with loud applause and cheering. More importantly, the listeners' approval was confirmed by subsequent large donations to the Nazi campaign war chest. After a series of elections, Hitler was appointed chancellor on 30 January 1933, going on to achieve total power as Führer (dictator) of Germany on 19 August 1934.

... If today the National Socialist Movement is regarded among widespread circles in Germany

as being hostile to our business life, I believe the reason for this view is to be found in the fact that we adopted towards the events which determined the development leading to our present position an attitude which differed from that of all the other organisations which are of any importance in our public life. Even now our outlook differs in many points from that of our opponents ...

I regard it as of the first importance to break once and for all with the view that our destiny is conditioned by world events. It is not true that our distress has its final cause in a world crisis, in a world catastrophe: the true view is that we have reached a state of general crisis, because from the first certain mistakes were made. I must not say 'According to the general view the Peace Treaty of Versailles is the cause of our misfortune' ...

It is also in my view false to say that life in Germany today is solely determined by considerations of foreign policy, that the primacy of foreign policy governs today the whole of our domestic life. Certainly a people can reach the point when foreign relations influence and determine completely its domestic life. But let no one say that such a condition is from the first either natural or desirable. Rather the important thing is that a people should create the conditions for a change in this state of affairs.

If anyone says to me that its foreign politics is primarily decisive for the life of a people, then I must first ask: what then is the meaning of the term 'politics'? There is a whole series of definitions. Frederick the Great said: 'Politics is the art of serving one's state with every means'. Bismarck's explanation was that 'Politics is the art of the possible', starting from the conception that advantage should be taken of every possibility to serve the state—and, in the later transformation of the idea of the state into the idea of nationalities, the nation. Another considers that this service rendered to the people can be effected by military as well as peaceful action, for Clausewitz says that war is the continuation of politics though with different means. Conversely, Clemenceau considers that today peace is nothing but the continuation of war and the pursuing of the war-aim, though again with other means ...

It is therefore false to say that foreign politics shapes a people: rather, peoples order their relations to the world about them in correspondence with their inborn forces and according to the measure in which their education enables them to bring those forces into play. We may be quite convinced that if in the place of the Germany of today there had stood a different Germany, the attitude towards the rest of the world would also have been different, and then presumably the influences exercised by the rest of the world would have taken a different form. To deny this would mean that Germany's destiny can no longer be changed no matter what government rules in Germany ...

And as against this conception I am the champion of another standpoint: three factors, I hold, essentially determine a people's political life:

First, the inner value of a people which as an inherited sum and possession is transmitted again and again through the generations, a value which suffers any change when the people, the custodian of this inherited possession, changes itself in its inner, blood-conditioned composition. It is beyond question that certain traits of character, certain virtues and certain vices always recur in peoples so long as their inner nature—their blood-conditioned composition—has not essentially altered. I can already trace the virtues and the vices of our German people in the writers of Rome just as clearly as I see them today. This inner value which determines the life of a people can be destroyed by nothing save only through a change in the blood causing a change in substance ...

I said that this value can be destroyed. There are indeed in especial two other closely related factors which we can time and again trace in periods of national decline: the one is that for the conception of the value of personality there is substituted a levelling idea of the supremacy of mere numbers—democracy—and the other is the negation of the value of a people, the denial of any difference in the inborn capacity, the achievement, etc, of individual peoples. Thus both factors condition one another or at least influence each other in the course of their development. Internationalism and democracy are inseparable conceptions. It is but logical that democracy, which within a people denies the special value of the individual and puts in its place a value which represents the sum of all individualities—a purely numerical value—should proceed in precisely the same way in the life of peoples and should in that sphere result in internationalism. Broadly it is maintained: peoples have no inborn values, but, at the most, there can be admitted perhaps temporary differences in education. Between negroes, Aryans, Mongolians and redskins there is no essential difference in value. This view which forms the basis of the whole of the international thought-world of today and in its effects is carried to such lengths that in the end a Negro can sit as president in the sessions of the League of Nations leads necessarily as a further consequence to the point that in a similar way within a people differences in value between the individual members of this people are denied. And thus naturally every special capacity, every fundamental value of a people, can practically be made of no effect. For the greatness of a people is the result not of the sum of all its achievements but in the last resort of the sum of its outstanding achievements ...

So it is only natural that when the capable intelligences of a nation, which are always in a minority, are regarded only as of the same value as all the rest, then genius, capacity, the value of personality are slowly subjected to the majority and this process is then falsely named the rule of the people. For this is not rule of the people, but in reality the rule of stupidity, of mediocrity, of half-heartedness, of cowardice, of weakness and of inadequacy ...

Thus democracy will in practice lead to the destruction of a people's true values ... And thus in these conditions a people will gradually lose its importance not merely in the cultural and economic spheres but altogether, in a comparatively short time it will no longer, within the setting of the other peoples of the world, maintain its former value ...

And to this there must be added a third factor: namely, the view that life in this world, after the denial of the value of personality and of the special value of a people, is not to be maintained through conflict. That is a conception which could perhaps be disregarded if it fixed itself only in the heads of individuals, but yet has appalling consequences because it slowly poisons an entire people. And it is not as if such general changes in men's outlook on the world remained only on the surface or were confined to their effects on men's minds. No, in the course of time they exercise a profound influence and affect all expressions of a people's life ...

To sum up the argument: I see two diametrically opposed principles: the principle of democracy which, wherever it is allowed practical effect is the principle of destruction: and the principle of the authority of personality which I would call the principle of achievement, because whatever man in the past has achieved—all human civilisations—is conceivable only if the supremacy of this principle is admitted ...

We have a number of nations which through their inborn outstanding worth have fashioned for themselves a mode of life which stands in no relation to the life-space—the *Lebensraum*—which, in their thickly populated settlements, they inhabit. We have the so-called white race, which, since the collapse of ancient civilisation, in the course of some thousand years has created for itself a privileged position in the world. But I am quite unable to understand this privileged position, this economic supremacy, of the white race over the rest of the world if I do not bring it into close connection with a political conception of supremacy which has been peculiar to the white race for many centuries and has been regarded as in the nature of things: this conception it has maintained in its dealings with other peoples. Take any single area you like, take for example India. England did not conquer India by the way of justice and of law: she conquered India without regard to the wishes, to the views of the natives, or to their formulations of justice, and, when necessary, she has upheld this supremacy with the most brutal ruthlessness …

If I think away this attitude of mind which in the course of the last three or four centuries has won the world for the white race, then the destiny of this race would in fact have been no different from that, say, of the Chinese: an immensely congested mass of human beings crowded upon an extraordinarily narrow territory, an over-population with all its unavoidable consequences. If fate allowed the white race to take a different path, that is only because this white race was convinced that it had the right to organise the rest of the world …

'Before the Gate of Germany Stands the New German Army'
Adolf Hitler, Nuremberg, Germany, 14 September 1936

By 1936, when he had been dictator for two years, Hitler decided that world domination was achievable. To that end, he prepared to devote Germany's entire industrial complex to the exclusive production of military hardware. As always, the rationale was that peaceful Germany was being forced (reluctantly) to defend itself against hostile opportunists of various persuasions. The demons in this speech are bolshevism (communism) and democracy, with the occasional reference to Jews, who, he claimed, invented both ideologies.

'Democracy is the canal through which bolshevism lets its poisons flow' was probably news to everyone outside Germany (and many inside), but one may admire the seductively poetic polemic. This speech, as always, is full of Hitler's self-referential logic, whereby his own motives are sublimated into his attacks on his enemies. And who could disagree with, 'That one should refuse to see a thing does not mean that it is not there', or 'He who is undertaking such great economic and cultural tasks as we are and is so determined to carry them through can find his fairest memorial only in peace'?

... I can come to no terms with a *Weltanschauung* [world view] which everywhere as its first act after gaining power is—not the liberation of the working people—but the liberation of the scum of humanity, the asocial creatures concentrated in the prisons—and then the letting loose of these wild beasts upon the terrified and helpless world about them ...

Bolshevism turns flourishing countrysides into sinister wastes of ruins; National Socialism transforms a Reich of destruction and misery into a healthy state and a flourishing economic life ...

Russia planned a world revolution and German workmen would be used but as cannon fodder for bolshevist imperialism. But we National Socialists do not wish that our military resources should be employed to impose by force on other peoples what those peoples themselves do not want. Our army does not swear on oath that it will with bloodshed extend the National Socialist idea over other peoples, but that it will with its own blood defend the National Socialist idea and thereby the German Reich, its security and freedom, from the aggression of other peoples ...

These are only some of the grounds for the antagonisms which separate us from communism. I confess, these antagonisms cannot be bridged. Here are really two worlds which do but grow further apart from each other and can never unite. When in an English newspaper a Parliamentarian complains that we wish to divide Europe into two parts, then unfortunately we are bound to inform this Robinson Crusoe living on his happy British island that—however unwelcome it may be—this division is already an accomplished fact ... That one should refuse to see a thing does not mean that it is not there. For many a year in Germany I have been laughed to scorn as a prophet; for many a year my warnings and my prophecies were regarded as the illusions of a mind diseased ...

Bolshevism has attacked the foundations of our whole human order, alike in state and society, the foundations of our conception of civilisation, of our faith and of our morals: all alike are at stake ...

Unfortunately I cannot escape the impression that most of those who doubt the danger to the world of bolshevism come themselves from the East. As yet politicians in England have not come to know bolshevism in their own country; we know it already. Since I have fought against these Jewish Soviet ideas in Germany, since I have conquered and stamped out this peril, I fancy that I possess a better comprehension of its character than do men who have only at best had to deal with it in the field of literature ... have won my successes simply because in the first place I endeavoured to see things as they are and not as one would like them to be; secondly, when once I had formed my own opinion I never allowed weaklings to talk me out of it or to cause me to abandon it; and thirdly, because I was always determined in all circumstances to yield to a necessity when once it had been recognised ...

It is not necessary for me to strengthen the fame of the National Socialist Movement, far less that of the German Army, through military triumphs. He who is undertaking such great economic and cultural tasks as we are and is so determined to carry them through can find his fairest memorial only in peace ... But this bolshevism which as we learned only a few months since intends to equip its army so that it may with violence, if necessary, open the gate to revolution among other peoples—this bolshevism should know that before the gate of Germany stands the new German Army ...

It is with grave anxiety that I see the possibility in Europe of some such development as this: democracy may continuously disintegrate the European states, may make them internally ever more uncertain in their judgment of the dangers which confront them, may above all cripple all power for resolute resistance. Democracy is the canal through which bolshevism lets its poisons flow into the separate countries and lets them work there long enough for these infections to lead to a crippling of intelligence and of the force of resistance. I regard it as possible that then—in order to avoid something still worse—coalition governments, masked as popular fronts or the like, will be formed and that these will endeavour to destroy—and perhaps will successfully destroy—in these peoples the last forces which remain, either in organisation or in mental outlook, which could offer opposition to bolshevism.

The brutal mass slaughters of National Socialist fighters, the burning of the wives of National Socialist officers after petrol had been poured over them, the massacre of children and of babies of National Socialist parents, for example in Spain, are intended to serve as a warning to forces in other lands which represent views akin to those of National Socialism. Such forces are to be intimidated so that in a similar position they offer no resistance. If these methods are successful: if the modern Girondins are succeeded by Jacobins, if Kerensky's popular front gives place to the bolshevists, then Europe will sink into a sea of blood and mourning ...

FIGHTING SONG

Lili Marlene

Underneath the lantern by the barrack gate,
Darling I remember
The way you used to wait,
'Twas there that you whispered tenderly,
That you loved me,
You'd always be,
My Lili of the lamplight,
My own Lili Marlene.

Time would come for roll call,
Time for us to part,
Darling I'd caress you and
Press you to my heart,
And there 'neath that far off lantern light,
I'd hold you tight,
We'd kiss good-night,
My Lili of the lamplight,
My own Lili Marlene.

Orders came for sailing
Somewhere over there,

All confined to barracks
Was more than I could bear;
I knew you were waiting in the street,
I heard your feet,
But could not meet,
My Lili of the lamplight,
My own Lili Marlene.

Resting in a billet
Just behind the line,
Even though we're parted
Your lips are close to mine,
You wait where that lantern softly gleams,
Your sweet face seems to haunt my dreams,
My Lili of the lamplight,
My own Lili Marlene.

'Lili Marlene' was originally a German song based on a poem written by German soldier Hans Leip in 1915. Norbert Schultze set the poem to music in 1938 and it was released just before the Second World War. It became a favourite of German troops, and its popularity led to a hurried English rewrite by Tommie Connor ('Till the Lights of London Shine Again'). Soon both sides were broadcasting their versions.

'Peace for Our Time'
Neville Chamberlain, London, 30 September 1938

Neville Chamberlain (1869–1940) was elected as British prime minister in 1937. He is, perhaps rather unfairly, best remembered for his policy of 'appeasement' with Germany and Italy leading up to the Second World War, and indeed he was anxious to avoid the bloodshed of the First World War and had some sympathy for Germany, believing that the terms of the 1919 Versailles Treaty were too severe.

In September 1938, Chamberlain met with Hitler, Mussolini and the French prime minister, Édouard Daladier, in Munich, where they agreed that Germany should annexe the Sudetenland region of Czechoslovakia. Hitler agreed not to make any further territorial claims but already had quite different plans in train. Chamberlain apparently took Hitler's assurances at face value, and returned triumphantly to England on 30 September. Waving the signed resolution in his hand, Chamberlain made the following statement on the tarmac of Heston Aerodrome.

We, the German Führer and Chancellor, and the British Prime Minister, have had a further meeting today and are agreed in recognising that the question of Anglo–German relations is of the first importance for the two countries and for Europe.

We regard the agreement signed last night and the Anglo–German Naval Agreement as symbolic of the desire of our two peoples never to go to war with one another again.

We are resolved that the method of consultation shall be the method adopted to deal with any other questions that may concern our two countries, and we are determined to continue our efforts to remove possible sources of difference, and thus to contribute to assure the peace of Europe.

Chamberlain later read the following statement:

My good friends, for the second time in our history a British prime minister has returned from Germany bringing peace with honour. I believe it is peace for our time. Go home and get a nice quiet sleep.

Declaration of War
Robert Menzies, Canberra, Australia, 3 September 1939

The first sentence of this radio speech by Prime Minister Robert Menzies (1894–1978) is part of Australian folklore, but it contains a misleading statement. When Menzies says, 'Great Britain has declared war upon (Germany) and that, as a result, Australia is also at war', he implies that Australia was obliged to support Britain, which was not true—no such formal treaty existed. Nonetheless, Australia's Parliament accepted Menzies' assumption.

Menzies' war legacy was mixed. In 1938, he had expressed admiration for the German government and allowed scrap iron to be sold to Japan, despite protests from dockers. During the war, he failed to obtain a commitment from Britain to come to Australia's aid in the event of a Japanese attack, as occurred in February 1942. His government disintegrated in October 1941 and was replaced by a Labor government led by John Curtin. Menzies, however, went on to found the Liberal Party, and served as prime minister from 1949 to 1966.

Fellow Australians, it is my melancholy duty to inform you officially that in consequence of a persistence by Germany in her invasion of Poland, Great Britain has declared war upon her and that, as a result, Australia is also at war.

No harder task can fall to the lot of a democratic leader than to make such an announcement. Great Britain and France, with the co-operation of the British Dominions, have struggled to avoid this tragedy. They have, as I firmly believe, been patient. They have kept the door of negotiation open. They have given no cause for aggression.

But in the result their efforts have failed and we are therefore, as a great family of nations, involved in a struggle which we must at all costs win and which we believe in our hearts we will win …

In the British government's communication of August 30, it informed the German Chancellor that it recognised the need for speed and that it also recognised the dangers which arose from the fact that two mobilised armies were facing each other on opposite sides of the Polish frontier, and that accordingly it strongly urged that both Germany and Poland should undertake that during the negotiations no aggressive military movements would take place. That being communicated to Poland, the Polish government on Thursday, August 31, categorically stated that it was prepared to give a formal guarantee that during negotiations Polish troops would not violate the frontiers, provided a corresponding guarantee was given by Germany. The German government made no reply whatever ...

If Germany had really desired a peaceful settlement ... she would have taken every step to see that her proposals were adequately considered by Poland and that there was proper opportunity for discussion. In other words, if Germany had wanted peace, does anybody believe that there would today be fighting on the Polish frontier, or that Europe would be plunged into war? Who wanted war? Poland? Great Britain? France?

I know that, in spite of the emotions we are all feeling, you will show that Australia is ready to see it through. May God in His mercy and compassion grant that the world may soon be delivered from this agony.

ROBERT MENZIES, 1939

Fireside Chat on the War in Europe
Franklin D. Roosevelt, Washington, D.C., 3 September 1939

Democrat leader Franklin Delano Roosevelt (1882–1945) was inaugurated US president in 1933. One of his methods of communicating with the population was by radio broadcasts, which he called 'fireside chats'. He used them to promote or defend policies, answer critics or build up national morale. This chat was broadcast a few hours after Great Britain and France declared war on Germany. Roosevelt emphasises the neutrality of the United States, but provides implicit support for the Allies. He is also softening the audience for his 21 September proposal, which would successfully call on Congress to permit the selling of arms to Great Britain and France.

Tonight my single duty is to speak to the whole of America.

Until 4.30 o'clock this morning I had hoped against hope that some miracle would prevent a devastating war in Europe and bring to an end the invasion of Poland by Germany.

For four long years a succession of actual wars and constant crises have shaken the entire world and have threatened in each case to bring on the gigantic conflict which is today unhappily a fact.

It is right that I should recall to your minds the consistent and at times successful efforts of your government in these crises to throw the full weight of the United States into the cause of peace. In spite of spreading wars I think that we have every right and every reason to maintain as a national policy the fundamental moralities, the teachings of religion and the continuation of efforts to restore peace. Because some day, though the time may be distant, we can be of even greater help to a crippled humanity ...

It is, of course, impossible to predict the future. I have my constant stream of information from American representatives and other sources throughout the world. You, the people of this country, are receiving news through your radios and your newspapers at every hour of the day.

You are, I believe, the most enlightened and the best-informed people in all the world at this moment. You are subjected to no censorship of news, and I want to add that your government has no information which it withholds or which it has any thought of withholding from you.

At the same time … it is of the highest importance that the press and the radio use the utmost caution to discriminate between actual verified fact on the one hand, and mere rumour on the other …

It is easy for you and for me to shrug our shoulders and to say that conflicts taking place thousands of miles from the continental United States, and, indeed, thousands of miles from the whole American hemisphere, do not seriously affect the Americas—and that all the United States has to do is to ignore them and go about its own business. Passionately though we may desire detachment, we are forced to realise that every word that comes through the air, every ship that sails the sea, every battle that is fought, does affect the American future. Let no man or woman thoughtlessly or falsely talk of America sending its armies to European fields. At this moment there is being prepared a proclamation of American neutrality. This … proclamation is in accordance with international law and in accordance with American policy.

This will be followed by a proclamation required by the existing Neutrality Act. And I trust that in the days to come our neutrality can be made a true neutrality ...

I myself cannot and do not prophesy the course of events abroad and the reason is that, because I have of necessity such a complete picture of what is going on in every part of the world, I do not dare to do so. And the other reason is that I think it is honest for me to be honest with the people of the United States.

I cannot prophesy the immediate economic effect of this new war on our nation, but I do say that no American has the moral right to profiteer at the expense either of his fellow citizens or of the men, the women and the children who are living and dying in the midst of war in Europe ...

We have certain ideas and certain ideals of national safety, and we must act to preserve that safety today, and to preserve the safety of our children in future years.

That safety is and will be bound up with the safety of the Western Hemisphere and of the seas adjacent thereto. We seek to keep war from our own firesides by keeping war from coming to the

Americas. For that we have historic precedent that goes back to the days of the administration of President George Washington. It is serious enough and tragic enough to every American family in every State in the Union to live in a world that is torn by wars on other continents. Those wars today affect every American home. It is our national duty to use every effort to keep those wars out of the Americas ...

This nation will remain a neutral nation, but I cannot ask that every American remain neutral in thought as well. Even a neutral has a right to take account of facts. Even a neutral cannot be asked to close his mind or his conscience.

I have said not once, but many times, that I have seen war and that I hate war. I say that again and again.

I hope the United States will keep out of this war. I believe that it will. And I give you assurance and reassurance that every effort of your government will be directed towards that end.

As long as it remains within my power to prevent, there will be no blackout of peace in the United States.

WAR CRIES

'Tora, Tora, Tora!' (Tiger, Tiger, Tiger!)
Coded signal indicating that the bombing of Pearl Harbor had been successful. Not, strictly speaking, a war cry, but sometimes mistaken for one.

'Ura!' (Hurrah!)
Russian army battle cry, pronounced 'Oo-rah' and probably derived from Turkish. Many cultures use a similar shout, although origins vary. US marines also shout 'Oo-rah!' but the root is different. The US Army shouts 'Hoo-ah!' US Navy teams yell 'Hoo-YAH!' for inspiration. The Argentine navy shouts 'Ua! Ua! Ua!', while the Greek army uses 'Aera!' ('Wind!', as in 'Blow them away like the …').

'Banzai!' (Ten thousand years!)
The battle cry of Japanese kamikaze pilots. Adapted from the Chinese 'Wansui!', this term has been used for over 1200 years to bless East Asian emperors. It is usually translated as 'Long live', although it contains extra, non-English cultural undertones— 'ten thousand' in Chinese and Japanese has an implication of infinity, much like the Greek myriad.

Radio Address to the German People
Neville Chamberlain, London, 4 September 1939

This speech was delivered when Chamberlain realised the error of his 'peace for our time' statement (see p. 116). Though Chamberlain is usually seen as an 'appeaser', many historians now believe he was aware of Hitler's aims and that his concession at Munich was a calculated tactic to buy Britain time to attain military superiority. Chamberlain resigned as prime minister in 1940, and was succeeded by Winston Churchill. He died a month later.

German people, your country and mine are at war. Your government has bombed and invaded the free and independent state of Poland, which this country is in honour bound to defend ... God knows this country has done everything possible to prevent this calamity. But now that the invasion of Poland by Germany has taken place, it has become inevitable.

You were told by your government that you are fighting because Poland rejected your leader's

offer and resorted to force. What are the facts? The so-called 'offer' was made to the Polish ambassador on Thursday evening, two hours before the announcement by your government that it had been 'rejected'. So far from having been rejected, there had been no time even to consider it. Your government had previously demanded that a Polish representative should be sent to Berlin within twenty-four hours to conclude an agreement. The Polish representative was expected to arrive within a fixed time to sign an agreement which he had not even seen. This is not negotiation. This is a dictate. To such methods no self-respecting and powerful state could assent. Negotiations on a free and equal basis might well have settled the matter in dispute.

You may ask why Great Britain is concerned. We are concerned because we gave our word of honour to defend Poland against aggression. Why did we feel it necessary to pledge ourselves to defend this eastern power when our interests lie in the west? The answer is— and I regret to have to say it—that nobody in this country any longer places any trust in your leader's word.

He gave his word that he would respect the Locarno Treaty; he broke it. He gave his word that he neither wished nor intended to annex Austria; he broke it. He declared that he would not incorporate the Czechs in the Reich; he did so. He gave his word after Munich that he had no further territorial demands in Europe; he broke it. He has sworn for years that he was the mortal enemy of bolshevism; he is now its ally.

Can you wonder his word is, for us, not worth the paper it is written on?

The German–Soviet Pact was a cynical volte-face, designed to shatter the Peace Front against aggression. This gamble failed. The Peace Front stands firm. Your leader is now sacrificing you, the German people, to the still more monstrous gamble of a war to extricate himself from the impossible position into which he has led himself and you.

In this war we are not fighting against you, the German people, for whom we have no bitter feeling, but against a tyrannous and forsworn regime which has betrayed not only its own people but the whole of western civilisation and all that you and we hold dear.

May God defend the right!

'We Shall Never Surrender'
Winston Churchill, London, 4 June 1940

One of the most famous pronouncements of Winston Churchill (1874–1965), this speech was made in the British House of Commons just after the evacuation of some 338,000 Allied troops from Dunkirk (Dunkerque), France, to England, and in the face of an impending German invasion.

By this time, German forces were occupying most of Europe, including France, Belgium and the Netherlands, just across the English Channel. The withdrawal from Dunkirk was successful, despite some 30,000 Allied casualties. The prime minister's inspiring speech boosted the morale of the British populace, and made a powerful plea for assistance from the still neutral United States.

From the moment when the defences at Sedan on the Meuse were broken at the end of the second week of May, only a rapid retreat to Amiens and the south could have saved the British and French armies who had entered Belgium at the appeal of the Belgian King.

This strategic fact was not immediately realised. The French high command hoped it would be able to close the gap. The armies of the north were under their orders. Moreover, a retirement of that kind would have involved almost certainly the destruction of a fine Belgian Army of twenty divisions and abandonment of the whole of Belgium.

Therefore, when the force and scope of the German penetration was realised and when the new French Generalissimo, General Weygand, assumed command in place of General Gamelin, an effort was made by the French and British armies in Belgium to keep holding the right hand of the Belgians and give their own right hand to the newly created French Army which was to advance across the Somme in great strength.

However, the German eruption swept like a sharp scythe south of Amiens to the rear of the armies in the north—eight or nine armoured divisions, each with about 400 armoured vehicles of different kinds divisible into small self-contained units. This force cut off all communications between us and the main French Army. It severed our communications for food and ammunition. It ran first through Amiens, afterwards through Abbeville, and along the coast to Boulogne and Calais, almost to Dunkerque.

Behind this armoured and mechanised onslaught came a number of German divisions in lorries, and behind them, again, plodded comparatively slowly the dull, brute mass of the ordinary German Army and German people, always ready to be led to the trampling down in other lands of liberties and comforts they never have known in their own ...

When a week ago today I asked the House to fix this afternoon for the occasion of a statement, I feared it would be my hard lot to announce from this box the greatest military disaster of our long history ...

I asked the House a week ago to suspend its judgment because the facts were not clear. I do not think there is now any reason why we should not form our own opinions upon this pitiful episode. The surrender of the Belgian Army compelled the British Army at the shortest notice to cover a flank to the sea of more than 30 miles' [48 kilometres'] length which otherwise would have been cut off.

In doing this and closing this flank, contact was lost inevitably between the British and two of three corps forming the First French Army who were then further from the coast than we were. It seemed impossible that large numbers of Allied troops could reach the coast. The enemy attacked on all sides in great strength and fierceness, and their main power, air force, was thrown into the battle.

The enemy began to fire cannon along the beaches by which alone shipping could approach or depart. They sowed magnetic mines in the channels and seas and sent repeated waves of hostile aircraft, sometimes more than one hundred strong, to cast bombs on a single pier that remained and on the sand dunes.

Their U-boats, one of which was sunk, and motor launches took their toll of the vast traffic which now began. For four or five days the intense struggle raged. All armoured divisions, or what was left of them, together with great masses of German infantry and artillery, hurled themselves on the ever narrowing and contracting appendix within which the British and French armies fought.

Meanwhile the Royal Navy, with the willing help of countless merchant seamen and a host of volunteers, strained every nerve and every effort and every craft to embark the British and Allied troops.

Over 220 light warships and more than 650 other vessels were engaged. They had to approach this difficult coast, often in adverse weather, under an almost ceaseless hail of bombs and increasing concentration of artillery fire. Nor were the seas themselves free from mines and torpedoes ...

Hospital ships, which were plainly marked, were the special target for Nazi bombs, but the men and women aboard them never faltered in their duty.

Meanwhile the RAF [Royal Air Force], who already had been intervening in the battle so far as its range would allow it to go from home bases, now used a part of its main metropolitan fighter strength to strike at German bombers.

The struggle was protracted and fierce. Suddenly the scene has cleared. The crash and thunder has momentarily, but only for the moment, died away. The miracle of deliverance

WINSTON CHURCHILL, 1940

achieved by the valour and perseverance, perfect discipline, faultless service, skill and unconquerable vitality is a manifesto to us all.

The enemy was hurled back by the British and French troops. He was so roughly handled that he dare not molest their departure seriously. The air force decisively defeated the main strength of the German Air Force and inflicted on them a loss of at least four to one ...

How long it will be, how long it will last depends upon the exertions which we make on this island. An effort, the like of which has never been seen in our records, is now being made. Work is proceeding night and day. Sundays and weekdays. Capital and labour have cast aside their interests, rights and customs and put everything into the common stock. Already the flow of munitions has leaped forward. There is no reason why we should not in a few months overtake the sudden and serious loss that has come upon us without retarding the development of our general program ...

The French Army has been weakened, the Belgian Army has been lost and a large part of those fortified lines upon which so much faith was reposed has gone, and many valuable mining districts and factories have passed into the enemy's possession.

The whole of the Channel ports are in his hands, with all the strategic consequences that follow from that, and we must expect another blow to be struck almost immediately at us or at France.

We were told that Hitler has plans for invading the British Isles. This has often been thought of before. When Napoleon lay at Boulogne for a year with his flat-bottomed boats and his Grand Army, someone told him there were bitter weeds in England. There certainly were and a good many more of them have since been returned. The whole question of defence against invasion is powerfully affected by the fact that we have for the time being in this island incomparably more military forces than we had in the last war. But this will not continue. We shall not be content with a defensive war. We have our duty to our Allies …

Turning once again, and this time more generally, to the question of invasion, I would observe that there has never been a period in all these long centuries of which we boast when an absolute guarantee against invasion, still less against serious raids, could have been given to our people. In the days of Napoleon the same wind which would have carried his transports across the Channel might have driven away the blockading fleet. There was always the chance, and it is that chance which has excited and befooled the imaginations of many continental tyrants. Many are the tales that are told. We are assured that novel methods will be adopted, and when we see the originality of malice, the ingenuity of aggression, which our enemy displays, we may certainly prepare ourselves for every kind of novel stratagem and every kind of brutal and treacherous manoeuvre. I think that no idea is so outlandish that it should not be considered and viewed with a searching, but at the same time, I hope, with a steady eye. We must never forget the solid assurances of sea power and those which belong to air power if it can be locally exercised.

I have, myself, full confidence that if all do their duty, if nothing is neglected, and if the best arrangements are made, as they are being made, we shall prove ourselves once again able to defend our island home, to ride out the storm of war, and to outlive the menace of tyranny, if necessary for years, if necessary alone. At any rate, that is what we are going to try to do …

Even though large tracts of Europe and many old and famous states have fallen or may fall into the grip of the Gestapo and all the odious apparatus of Nazi rule, we shall not flag or fail. We shall go on to the end, we shall fight in France, we shall fight on the seas and oceans, we shall fight with growing confidence and growing strength in the air, we shall defend our island, whatever the cost may be, we shall fight on the beaches, we shall fight on the landing grounds, we shall fight in the fields and in the streets, we shall fight in the hills; we shall never surrender, and even if, which I do not for a moment believe, this island or a large part of it were subjugated and starving, then our Empire beyond the seas, armed and guarded by the British Fleet, would carry on the struggle, until, in God's good time, the New World, with all its power and might, steps forth to the rescue and the liberation of the old.

WINSTON CHURCHILL

'You were given the choice between war and dishonour. You chose dishonour and you will have war.'
Churchill on Neville Chamberlain and his appeasement policy, 1938

'I cannot forecast to you the action of Russia. It is a riddle wrapped in a mystery inside an enigma.'
Speech broadcast in October 1939

'If Hitler were to invade hell, I should find occasion to make a favourable reference to the Devil in the House of Commons.'
Fervent anticommunist and Stalin-hater Churchill explains why Britain will support the Soviet Union after the German invasion of June 1941

'Never give in—never, never, never, never … never give in except to convictions of honour and good sense.'
Speech given at Harrow School, 29 October 1941

'This Was Their Finest Hour'
Winston Churchill, London, 18 June 1940

This speech to the House of Commons was made a week after the French surrender, as Britain continued to face invasion. Churchill correctly predicts that the German attack would be mainly from the air, and that the Royal Air Force (RAF) would 'have the glory of saving their native land'. The Germans greatly underestimated the strength of the RAF, losing more than 1600 aircraft to Britain's 1087 during the four-month battle. After failing to win the air war, in September Hitler ordered attacks on nonmilitary targets, in a misguided attempt to demoralise the population. Meanwhile, the British were building new aircraft at double the German rate. Later, after Britain's successful repulsion of the German attack, Churchill would say of the RAF: 'Never in the field of human conflict was so much owed by so many to so few'.

… During the great battle in France, we gave very powerful and continuous aid to the French Army, both by fighters and bombers;

but in spite of every kind of pressure we never would allow the entire metropolitan fighter strength of the Air Force to be consumed. This decision was painful, but it was also right, because the fortunes of the battle in France could not have been decisively affected even if we had thrown in our entire fighter force. That battle was lost by the unfortunate strategical opening, by the extraordinary and unforeseen power of the armoured columns, and by the great preponderance of the German Army in numbers. Our fighter Air Force might easily have been exhausted as a mere accident in that great struggle, and then we should have found ourselves at the present time in a very serious plight. But as it is, I am happy to inform the House that our fighter strength is stronger at the present time relative to the Germans, who have suffered terrible losses, than it has ever been; and consequently we believe ourselves possessed of the capacity to continue the war in the air under better conditions than we have ever experienced before. I look forward confidently to the exploits of our fighter pilots, these splen-did men, this brilliant youth, who will have the glory of saving their native land, their island home and all they love, from the most deadly of all attacks …

We do not yet know what will happen in France or whether the French resistance will be prolonged, both in France and in the French Empire overseas. The French government will be throwing away great opportunities and casting adrift their future if they do not continue the war in accordance with their treaty obligations, from which we have not felt able to release them. The House will have read the historic declaration in which, at the desire of many Frenchmen, and of our own hearts, we have proclaimed our willingness at the darkest hour in French history to conclude a union of common citizenship in this struggle. However matters may go in France or with the French government, or other French governments, we in this island and in the British Empire will never lose our sense of comradeship with the French people. If we are now called upon to endure what they have been suffering, we shall emulate their courage, and if final victory rewards our toils they shall share the gains, aye, and freedom shall be restored to all. We abate nothing of our just demands; not one jot or title do we recede. Czechs, Poles, Norwegians, Dutch, Belgians have joined their causes to our own. All these shall be restored.

What General Weygand called the Battle of France is over. I expect that the Battle of Britain is about to begin. Upon this battle depends the survival of Christian civilisation. Upon it depends our own British life and the long continuity of our institutions and our Empire. The whole fury and might of the enemy must very soon be turned on us now. Hitler knows that he will have to break us in this island or lose the war. If we can stand up to him, all Europe may be free and the life of the world may move forward into broad, sunlit uplands. But if we fail, then the whole world, including the United States, including all that we have known and cared for, will sink into the abyss of a new Dark Age, made more sinister, and perhaps more protracted, by the lights of perverted science. Let us therefore brace ourselves to our duties, and so bear ourselves that, if the British Empire and its Commonwealth last for a thousand years, men will still say, 'This was their finest hour'.

'We Are Merely Interested in Safeguarding Peace'
Adolf Hitler, Berlin, 4 May 1941

Hitler's use of the word 'peace' became more and more a staple of his speeches. In the 1920s and early 1930s he occasionally used the word to reproach his perceived enemies, but after 1936 it became something of a mantra, a repetitive cloak to deceive, and conceal, his decidedly unpeaceful plans. At the time of this speech, German troops already occupied Denmark, Norway, Poland, and most of Finland. France, Belgium, Luxembourg and the Netherlands had all been conquered within a month in the summer of 1940.

In this speech to the Reichstag, Hitler masquerades as a humanitarian peace-lover in the face of fanatical, ignorant and hostile opponents, and, as always, 'the great international Jewish financial interests that control the banks ... as well as the armament industry'. Ironically, he points to Winston Churchill as 'proof of that perpetual blindness with which the gods afflict those whom they are about to destroy'. Right idea; wrong person.

Deputies. Men of the German Reichstag:

At a time when only deeds count and words are of little importance, it is not my intention to appear before you, the elected representatives of the German people, more often than absolutely necessary. The first time I spoke to you was at the outbreak of the war when, thanks to the Anglo–French conspiracy against peace, every attempt at an understanding with Poland, which otherwise would have been possible, had been frustrated.

The most unscrupulous men of the present time had, as they admit today, decided as early as 1936 to involve the Reich, which in its peaceful work of reconstruction was becoming too powerful for them, in a new and bloody war and, if possible, to destroy it. They had finally succeeded in finding a state that was prepared for their interests and aims, and that state was Poland.

All my endeavours to come to an understanding with Britain were wrecked by the determination of a small clique which, whether from motives of hate or for the sake of material gain, rejected every German proposal for an understanding due to their resolve, which they never concealed, to resort to war, whatever happened.

The man behind this fanatical and diabolical plan to bring about war at whatever cost was Mr Churchill. His associates were the men who now form the British government.

These endeavours received most powerful support, both openly and secretly, from the so-called great democracies on both sides of the Atlantic. At a time when the people were more and more dissatisfied with their deficient statesmanship, the responsible men over there believed that a successful war would be the most likely means of solving problems that otherwise would be beyond their power to solve. Behind these men there stood the great international Jewish financial interests that control the banks and the stock exchange as well as the armament industry. And now, just as before, they scented the opportunity of doing their unsavoury business. And so, just as before, there was no scruple about sacrificing the blood of the peoples. That was the beginning of this war. A few weeks later the state that was the third country in Europe, Poland, but had been reckless enough to allow herself to be used for the financial interests of these warmongers, was annihilated and destroyed.

In these circumstances I considered that I owed it to our German people and countless men and women in the opposite camps ... to make yet another appeal to the commonsense and the conscience of these statesmen. On 6 October 1939, I therefore once more publicly stated that Germany had neither demanded nor intended to demand anything either from Britain or from France, that it was madness to continue the war and, above all, that the scourge of modern weapons of warfare, once they were brought into action, would inevitably ravage vast territories.

But just as the appeal I made on 1 September 1939 proved to be in vain, this renewed appeal met with indignant rejection. The British and their Jewish capitalist backers could find no other explanation for this appeal, which I had made on humanitarian grounds, than the assumption of weakness on the part of Germany.

They assured the people of Britain and France that Germany dreaded the clash to be expected in the spring of 1940 and was eager to make peace for fear of the annihilation that would then inevitably result ...

On 19 July 1940, I then convened the German Reichstag for the third time in order to render that great account which you all still remember. The meeting provided me with the opportunity of expressing the thanks of the nation to its soldiers in a form suited to the uniqueness of the event. Once again I seized the opportunity of urging the world to make peace. And what I foresaw and prophesied at that time happened. My offer of peace was misconstrued as a symptom of fear and cowardice.

The European and American warmongers succeeded once again in befogging the sound commonsense of the masses, who can never hope to profit from this war, by conjuring up false pictures of new hope. Thus, finally, under pressure of public opinion, as formed by their press, they once more managed to induce the nation to continue this struggle.

Even my warnings against night bombings of the civilian population, as advocated by Mr Churchill, were interpreted as a sign of German impotence. He, the most bloodthirsty or amateurish strategist that history has ever known, actually saw fit to believe that the reserve displayed for months by the German Air Force could be looked upon only as proof of their incapacity to fly by night ...

As a German and as a soldier I consider it unworthy ever to revile a fallen enemy. But it seems to me to be necessary to defend the truth from the wild exaggerations of a man who as a soldier is a bad politician and as a politician is an equally bad soldier.

Mr Churchill, who started this struggle, is endeavouring, as with regard to Norway or Dunkirk, to say something that sooner or later might perhaps be twisted around to resemble success. I do not consider that honourable but in his case it is understandable.

The gift Mr Churchill possesses is the gift to lie with a pious expression on his face and to distort the truth until finally glorious victories are made out of the most terrible defeats ... Churchill, one of the most hopeless dabblers in strategy ... who in any other country would be court-martialled, gained fresh admiration as prime minister, this cannot be construed as an expression of magnanimity such as was accorded by Roman senators to generals honourably defeated in battle. It is merely proof of that perpetual blindness with which the gods afflict those whom they are about to destroy …

Apart from the modest correction of its frontiers, which were infringed as a result of the outcome of the World War, the Reich has no special territorial interests in these parts. As far as politics are concerned we are merely interested in safeguarding peace in this region, while in the realm of economics we wish to see an order that will allow the production of goods to be developed and the exchange of products to be resumed in the interests of all. It is, however, only in accordance with supreme justice if those interests are also taken into account that are founded upon ethnographical, historical or economic conditions.

I can assure you that I look into the future with perfect tranquillity and great confidence. The German Reich and its allies represent power, military, economic and, above all, in moral respects, which is superior to any possible coalition in the world. The German armed forces will always do their part whenever it may be necessary. The confidence of the German people will always accompany their soldiers.

Reaction to the German Invasion of Russia

Vyacheslav Molotov, Moscow,
22 June 1941

A week before the German invasion of Poland, on 23 August 1939, Germany and Russia signed a non-aggression pact. Stalin kept his part of the deal, but on 22 June 1941, 3 million German and other Axis troops invaded Russia. At 5.30 am on 22 June, when Stalin received news of the German declaration of war (hours after the invasion had started), he was so stunned he said nothing to the populace. Finally, at noon the same day, the hesitant voice of foreign minister Vyacheslav Molotov (1890–1986) emerged from the radio.

Citizens of the Soviet Union, the Soviet government and its head, Comrade Stalin, have authorised me to make the following statement:

Today at 4 o'clock am, without any claims having been presented to the Soviet Union, without a declaration of war, German troops attacked our country, attacked our borders at

many points and bombed from their aeroplanes our cities; Zhitomir, Kiev, Sevastopol, Kaunas and some others, killing and wounding over 200 persons. There were also enemy air raids and artillery shelling from Romanian and Finnish territory.

This unheard of attack upon our country is perfidy unparalleled in the history of civilised nations. The attack on our country was perpetrated despite the fact that a treaty of nonaggression had been signed between the USSR and Germany and that the Soviet government most faithfully abided by all provisions of this treaty ...

The government of the Soviet Union expresses its unshakable confidence that our valiant army and navy and brave falcons of the Soviet Air Force will acquit themselves with honour in performing their duty to the fatherland and to the Soviet people, and will inflict a crushing blow upon the aggressor.

This is not the first time that our people have had to deal with an attack of an arrogant foe. At the time of Napoleon's invasion of Russia our people's reply was war for the fatherland, and Napoleon suffered defeat and met his doom.

It will be the same with Hitler, who in his arrogance has proclaimed a new crusade against our country. The Red Army and our whole people will again wage victorious war for the fatherland, for our country, for honour, for liberty.

The government of the Soviet Union expresses the firm conviction that the whole population of our country, all workers, peasants and intellectuals, men and women, will conscientiously perform their duties and do their work. Our entire people must now stand solid and united as never before.

Each one of us must demand of himself and of others discipline, organisation and self-denial worthy of real Soviet patriots, in order to provide for all the needs of the Red Army, Navy and Air Force, to insure victory over the enemy.

The government calls upon you, citizens of the Soviet Union, to rally still more closely around our glorious Bolshevist party, around our Soviet government, around our great leader and comrade, Stalin. Ours is a righteous cause. The enemy shall be defeated. Victory will be ours.

FAMOUS LAST WORDS

'I feel here that this time they have succeeded.'
Leon Trotsky (1879–1940), Russian revolutionary, pointing at his heart after an assassin delivered a fatal blow to his head with an ice-pick in Mexico City

'Es Lebe Die Freiheit!' (Long live freedom!)
Hans Scholl (1918–43), anti-Hitler resistance leader, before his execution for high treason

'My dear Melinée, my beloved little orphan, in a few hours I will no longer be of this world. We are going to be executed today at 3. This is happening to me like an accident in my life; I don't believe it, but I nevertheless know that I will never see you again.'
Missak Manouchian (1906–44), leader of the Parisian section of a communist Resistance movement, in a letter to his daughter before being executed by a German firing squad

'Shoot me in the chest!'
Benito Mussolini (1883–1945), Italian dictator, before his execution by communist Italian partisans

Declaration of War on Japan
Franklin D. Roosevelt,
Washington, D.C., 8 December 1941

President Roosevelt's speech to the US Congress, made the day after the attack on Pearl Harbor, was intended to evoke a stark emotional reaction. Roosevelt resolutely focused on the base ethical behaviour and character of the Japanese government, and spoke of the 'righteous might' of the American people.

The most famous line of the speech was originally 'a date which will live in world history'; Roosevelt replaced 'world history' with 'infamy'. This is a significant difference: it implies not just history, but the judgment of history in favour of America. It was a statement on behalf of the US population in the face of their communal distress.

Three days later, Germany and Italy declared war on the United States, and the European and South-East Asian wars became a worldwide conflict.

Yesterday, December 7, 1941—a date which will live in infamy—the United States of America

was suddenly and deliberately attacked by naval and air forces of the Empire of Japan.

The United States was at peace with that nation, and, at the solicitation of Japan, was still in conversation with its government and its Emperor looking towards the maintenance of peace in the Pacific.

Indeed, one hour after Japanese air squadrons had commenced bombing in the American island of Oahu, the Japanese Ambassador to the United States and his colleague delivered to our Secretary of State a formal reply to a recent American message. And, while this reply stated that it seemed useless to continue the existing diplomatic negotiations, it contained no threat or hint of war or of armed attack.

It will be recorded that the distance of Hawaii from Japan makes it obvious that the attack was deliberately planned many days or even weeks ago. During the intervening time the Japanese government has deliberately sought to deceive the United States by false statements and expressions of hope for continued peace.

The attack yesterday on the Hawaiian Islands has caused severe damage to American naval and military forces. I regret to tell you that very many American lives have been lost. In addition, American ships have been reported torpedoed on the high seas between San Francisco and Honolulu.

Yesterday the Japanese government also launched an attack against Malaya.

Last night Japanese forces attacked Hong Kong.

Last night Japanese forces attacked Guam.

Last night Japanese forces attacked the Philippine Islands.

Last night the Japanese attacked Wake Island.

And this morning the Japanese attacked Midway Island.

Japan has therefore undertaken a surprise offensive extending throughout the Pacific area. The facts of yesterday and today speak for themselves. The people of the United States have already formed their opinions and well understand the implications to the very life and safety of our nation.

As Commander-in-Chief of the Army and Navy I have directed that all measures be taken for our defence, that always will our whole nation remember the character of the onslaught against us.

No matter how long it may take us to overcome this premeditated invasion, the American people ... will win through to absolute victory ...

Our people, our territory and our interests are in grave danger.

With confidence in our armed forces, with the unbounding determination of our people, we will gain the inevitable triumph. So help us God.

I ask that the Congress declare that since the unprovoked and dastardly attack by Japan on Sunday, December 7, 1941, a state of war has existed between the United States and the Japanese empire.

'The Black of the Night Must Pass'
John Curtin, Canberra, Australia, 14 March & 17 April 1942

In October 1941, a Labor government, led by John Curtin (1885–1945), assumed office in Australia. Recognising the increasing danger of Japanese aggression, it assessed Australia's defences and soon realised they were almost nonexistent—most Australian troops were then fighting alongside the Allies in other parts of the world.

Focused on defeating the Nazis, Winston Churchill resisted the withdrawal of Australian troops from the Middle East. He also made a secret pact with President Roosevelt to commit US forces to the defence of Britain, which would have abandoned Asia and Australia to Japan (the plan was later overturned, however, on the advice of US military leaders).

On 26 December 1941, Curtin had said in a radio address, 'Without any inhibitions of any kind, I make it quite clear that Australia looks to America, free of any pangs as to our traditional links or kinship with the United Kingdom'. His comments caused uproar; Churchill sent him an angry cable, while Roosevelt, believing that Australia was a British colony, considered the comments treacherous. (After it was brought to his attention that Australia was actually an independent country, he came to respect Curtin's strong leadership.)

Curtin's radio address to America of 14 March 1942 marked the beginning of a sea change in the foreign policy of Australia, initiating a closer relationship with the United States that continues to this day. Nevertheless, on 17 April, Curtin made a similar address to the British people, asserting that Australia was still a staunch ally.

14 March 1942
Men and women of the United States:

I speak to you from Australia. I speak from a united people to a united people, and my speech is aimed to serve all the people of the nations united in the struggle to save mankind.

On the great waters of the Pacific Ocean war now breathes its bloody steam. From the skies of the Pacific pours down a deathly hail. In the countless islands of the Pacific the tide of war flows madly. For you in America; for us

in Australia, it is flowing badly. Let me then address you as comrades in this war and tell you a little of Australia and Australians. I am not speaking to your government. We have long been admirers of Mr Roosevelt and have the greatest confidence that he understands fully the critical situation in the Pacific and that America will go right out to meet it. For all that America has done, both before and after entering the war, we have the greatest admiration and gratitude.

It is to the people of America I am now speaking; to you who are, or will be, fighting; to you who are sweating in factories and workshops to turn out the vital munitions of war; to all of you who are making sacrifices in one way or another to provide the enormous resources required for our great task. I speak to you at a time when the loss of Java and the splendid resistance of the gallant Dutch together give us a feeling of both sadness and pride. Japan has moved one step further in her speedy march south; but the fight of the Dutch and Indonese in Java has shown that a brave, freedom-loving people are more than a match for the yellow aggressor given even a shadow below equality in striking and fighting weapons.

But facts are stern things. We, the Allied nations, were unready. Japan, behind her wall of secrecy, had prepared for war on a scale of which neither we nor you had knowledge. We have all made mistakes, we have all been too slow; we have all shown weakness—all the Allied nations. This is not the time to wrangle about who has been most to blame. Now our eyes are open.

The Australian government has fought for its people. We never regarded the Pacific as a segment of the great struggle. We did not insist that it was the primary theatre of war, but we did say, and events have so far, unhappily, proved us right, that the loss of the Pacific can be disastrous. Who among us, contemplating the future on that day in December last when Japan struck like an assassin at Pearl Harbor, at Manila, at Wake and Guam, would have hazarded a guess that by March the enemy would be astride all the southwest Pacific except General MacArthur's gallant men, and Australia and New Zealand. But that is the case. And, realising very swiftly that it would be the case, the Australian government sought a full and proper recognition of the part the Pacific was playing in the general strategic disposition of the world's warring forces. It was, therefore, but natural that, within twenty days after Japan's first treacherous blow, I said on behalf of the Australian government that we looked to America as the paramount factor on the democracies' side of the Pacific.

There is no belittling of the Old Country in this outlook. Britain has fought and won in the air the tremendous Battle of Britain. Britain has fought, and with your strong help, has won, the equally vital battle of the Atlantic. She has a paramount obligation to supply all possible help to Russia. She cannot, at the same time, go all out in the Pacific. We Australians, with New Zealand, represent Great Britain here in the Pacific—we are her sons—and on us the responsibility falls. I pledge to you my word we will not fail. You, as I have said, must be our leader. We will pull knee to knee with you for every ounce of our weight …

We are, then, committed, heart and soul, to total warfare. How far, you may ask me, have we progressed along that road? I may answer you this way. Out of every ten men in Australia four are wholly engaged in war as members of the fighting forces or making the munitions and equipment to fight with. The other six, besides feeding and clothing the whole ten and their families, have to produce the food and wool and metals which Britain needs for her very existence. We are not, of course, stopping at four out of ten. We had over three when Japan challenged our life and liberty. The proportion is now growing every day. On the one hand we are ruthlessly cutting out unessential expenditure so as to free men and women for war work; and on the other, mobilising woman-power to the utmost to supplement the men. From four out of ten devoted to war, we shall pass to five and six out of ten. We have no limit ...

I am not boasting to you. But were I to say less I would not be paying proper due to a band of men who have been tested in the crucible of world wars and hallmarked as pure metal. Our fighting forces and born attackers; we will hit the enemy wherever we can, as often as we can, and the extent of it will be measured only by the weapons in our hands ...

We fight with what we have and what we have is our all. We fight for the same free institutions that you enjoy. We fight so that, in the words of Lincoln, 'government of the people, for the people, by the people, shall not perish from the earth'. Our legislature is elected the same as is yours; and we will fight for it, and for the right to have it, just as you will fight to keep the Capitol at Washington the meeting place of freely elected men and women representative of a free people.

But I give you this warning: Australia is the last bastion between the west coast of America and the Japanese. If Australia goes, the Americas are wide open. It is said that the Japanese will bypass Australia and that they can be met and routed in India. I say to you that the saving of Australia is the saving of America's west coast. If you believe anything to the contrary then you delude yourselves.

Be assured of the calibre of our national character. This war may see the end of much that we have painfully and slowly built in our 150 years of existence. But even though all of it go, there will still be Australians fighting on Australian soil until the turning point be reached, and we will advance over blackened ruins, through blasted and fire-swept cities, across scorched plains, until we drive the enemy into the sea. I give you the pledge of my country. There will always be an Australian government and there will always be an Australian people. We are too strong in our hearts; our spirit is too high; the justice of our cause throbs too deeply in our being for that high purpose to be overcome.

I may be looking down a vista of weary months; of soul-shaking reverses; of grim struggle; of backbreaking work. But as surely as I sit here talking to you across the war-tossed Pacific Ocean I see our flag; I see Old Glory; I see the proud banner of the heroic Chinese; I see the standard of the valiant Dutch.

And I see them flying high in the wind of liberty over a Pacific from which aggression has been wiped out; over peoples restored to freedom; and flying triumphant as the glorified symbols of united nations strong in will and in power to achieve decency and dignity, unyielding to evil in any form.

JOHN CURTIN, 1942

17 April 1942

Fellow Britishers,

At this time of crisis and trial, with dark forebodings of things to come, I bring to you a message from Australia. A message not of mere words, but a factual statement of what we, in a Dominion of the British Commonwealth, are doing, and will do, so that your heroic struggle will be made easier and the ultimate victory so much swifter.

I will not dwell on what you have gone through in the past. That is a story of human gallantry, stoic courage and grim determination unparalleled in history. It throbs our hearts with pride and gratitude. We say to you that we have taken a pattern from it. In Australia we have made up our minds that no sacrifice can be too great; no effort shall be beyond our ability; and no obstacle shall daunt us in ensuring that Australia's part in the Battle of Britain will be faithfully and inflexibly honoured ...

In this war, as you well know, the backbone of the nation is in the workshop and in the factory. The workers of Australia have made that backbone a very real thing and they have done so because they have a wholesale conviction of the justice of Britain's cause. They are with you in this struggle because they are assured that everything they regard as being worthwhile is at stake. Bone of your bone, the workers of Australia are kindred. They are of your stock. Their forebears came from England, and from Ireland, and from Scotland, and from Wales. They inherit the ties of blood and grace and tongue that have joined British people together for centuries. Australia is a British land of one race and one tongue. It is a land in which people came from the British Isles to carve out for themselves, in freedom and equality, an opportunity to make for themselves and their children a better and freer life. That opportunity and the opportunity to aspire to even better things are still here. We are not going to allow our hopes to be thrust aside by any doctrine of repression and any doctrine which abnegates human rights.

Australians feel that they are playing their part. Australians are modestly proud of what our soldiers and airmen in the Middle East have achieved. We are proud of what our navy has done and we are bringing the production of raw materials and manufactured materials very swiftly to a maximum so that Britain, as far as Australia is concerned, at least will not lack. We have our own problems and the working out of the tangled skein of ambitions and counter ambitions in the Pacific involves us very deeply.

Our position in the Pacific is shortly stated. We do not want war here. We believe that aggression should play no part in the policies of the peoples of the Pacific. Nevertheless, we will resist aggression and, just as you, our kinsmen in Britain, stand to arms in defence of those fair isles, so also do we stand ready to keep war out of Australia.

Be of good cheer. The black of the night must pass into the brightness of morning; a morning for a new world in which human freedoms will be the paramount factor. Australian labour sends a comradely message of united endeavour to British labour. Australia sends to Great Britain her unflinching devotion and her steadfastness in the belief that victory must come in the battle for all that is meant in the word freedom. Good luck to you all.

FIGHTING WORDS

'What difference does it make to the dead, the orphans and the homeless, whether the mad destruction is wrought under the name of totalitarianism or the holy name of liberty and democracy?'

Mohandas Gandhi (1869–1948), peace activist

'Never think that war, no matter how necessary, nor how justified, is not a crime.'

Ernest Hemingway (1899–1961), US author

'War is not an adventure. It is a disease. It is like typhus.'

Antoine de Saint Exupéry (1900–44), French aviator and writer

'You can no more win a war than you can win an earthquake.'

Jeannette Rankin (1880–1973), US politician

'When the rich wage war, it's the poor who die.'

Jean-Paul Sartre (1905–80), French philosopher, dramatist, novelist and critic

Speech to the US Third Army
General George S. Patton, England, May and June 1944

This inspirational speech is unusual in that it was not broadcast or recorded; it was a private pep talk to US troops, delivered to several different audiences in the weeks leading up to the successful Allied D-Day invasion of France on 6 June 1944. The language is very earthy; even so, we may assume that it has been cleaned up. In 1951, the *New American Mercury* magazine printed a version of the speech, which had originally appeared in the *New York Daily News* on 31 May 1945. After publication, the magazine received so many requests for reprints that the editors decided to make a recording of the speech. Despite there being no legal obligation to do so, they asked Patton's widow Beatrice for her blessing. However, as the *Mercury* editors said:

Mrs Patton considered the matter graciously and thoroughly, and gave us a disappointing decision. She took the position that this speech was made by the General only to the men who were going to fight and die with him; it was, therefore, not a speech for the public or for posterity. We think Mrs Patton is wrong; we think that what is great and worth preserving about General Patton was expressed in that invasion speech. The fact that he employed four-letter words was proper; four-letter words are the language of war; without them wars would be quite impossible.

The project was then abandoned.

When Patton's nephew and biographer Fred Ayer Jr asked him about his use of profanity, Patton said: 'When I want my men to remember something important, to really make it stick, I give it to them double dirty … An army without profanity couldn't fight its way out of a piss-soaked paper bag'.

A lifelong soldier, Patton (1885–1945) joined the US Regular Army in 1909. He served in the First World War, rising to the rank of Lieutenant Colonel in 1918, and in the Second World War he commanded armies in Europe and North Africa, receiving numerous military awards. Historians consider him a brilliant military leader whose record was tarnished by disobedience and rash conduct.

Be seated. Men, this stuff that some sources sling around about America wanting out of this war, not wanting to fight, is a crock of bull****. Americans love to fight, traditionally. All real Americans love the sting and clash of battle.

You are here today for three reasons. First, because you are here to defend your homes and your loved ones. Second, you are here for your own self-respect, because you would not want to be anywhere else. Third, you are here because you are real men and all real men like to fight. When you, here, every one of you, were kids, you all admired the champion marble player, the fastest runner, the toughest boxer, the big league ball players, and the All-American football players. Americans love a winner. Americans will not tolerate a loser. Americans despise cowards. Americans play to win all of the time. I wouldn't give a hoot in hell for a man who lost and laughed. That's why Americans have never lost nor will ever lose a war; for the very idea of losing is hateful to an American.

You are not all going to die. Only two per cent of you right here today would die in a major battle. Death must not be feared. Death, in time, comes to all men. Yes, every man is scared in his first battle. If he says he's not, he's a liar. Some men are cowards but they fight the same as the brave men or they get the hell slammed out of them watching men fight who are just as scared as they are. The real hero is the man who fights even though he is scared. Some men get over their fright in a minute under fire. For some, it takes an hour. For some, it takes days. But a real man will never let his fear of death overpower his honour, his sense of duty to his country, and his innate manhood. Battle is the most magnificent competition in which a human being can indulge. It brings out all that is best and it removes all that is base. Americans pride themselves on being he-men and they ARE he-men.

Remember that the enemy is just as frightened as you are, and probably more so. They are not supermen. All through your army careers, you men have bitched about what you call 'chicken s*** drilling'. That, like everything else in this army, has a definite purpose. That purpose is alertness. Alertness must be bred into every soldier. I don't give a f*** for a man who's not always on his toes.

You men are veterans or you wouldn't be here. You are ready for what's to come. A man must be alert at all times if he expects to stay alive. If you're not alert, sometime, a German son-of-an-a**hole-bitch is going to sneak up behind you and beat you to death with a sock full of s***! There are 400 neatly marked graves somewhere in Sicily, all because one man went to sleep on the job. But they are German graves, because we caught the bastard asleep before they did.

An army is a team. It lives, sleeps, eats and fights as a team. This individual heroic stuff is pure horses***. The bilious bastards who write that kind of stuff for the *Saturday Evening Post* don't know any more about real fighting under fire than they know about f***ing! We have the finest food, the finest equipment, the best spirit and the best men in the world. Why, by God, I actually pity those poor sons-of-bitches we're going up against. By God, I do. My men don't surrender, and I don't want to hear of any soldier under my command being captured unless he has been hit. Even if you are hit, you can still fight back. That's not just bulls*** either. The kind of man that I want in my command is just like the lieutenant in Libya, who, with a Luger against his chest, jerked off his helmet, swept the gun aside with one hand, and busted the hell out of the Kraut with his helmet. Then he jumped on the gun and went out and killed another German before they knew what the hell was coming off. And, all of that time, this man had a bullet through a lung. There was a real man!

All of the real heroes are not storybook combat fighters, either. Every single man in this army plays a vital role. Don't ever let up. Don't ever think that your job is unimportant. Every man has a job to do and he must do it. Every man is a vital link in the great chain. What if every truck driver suddenly decided that he didn't like the whine of those shells overhead, turned yellow, and jumped headlong into a ditch? The cowardly bastard could say, 'Hell, they won't miss me, just one man in thousands'. But, what if every man thought that way? Where in the hell would we be now? What would our country, our loved ones, our homes, even the world, be like? No, goddamn it, Americans don't think like that. Every man does his job. Every man serves the whole. Every department, every unit, is important in the vast scheme of this war. The ordnance men are needed to supply the guns and machinery of war to keep us rolling. The quartermaster is needed to bring up food and clothes because where we are going there isn't a hell of a lot to steal. Every last man on KP [kitchen patrol] has a job to do, even the one who heats our water to keep us from getting the 'GI S***s'.

Each man must not think only of himself, but also of his buddy fighting beside him. We don't want yellow cowards in this army. They should be killed off like rats. If not, they will go home after this war and breed more cowards. The brave men will breed more brave men. Kill off the goddamned cowards and we will have a nation of brave men. One of the bravest men that I ever saw was a fellow on top of a telegraph pole in the midst of a furious firefight in Tunisia. I stopped and asked what the hell he was doing up there at a time like that. He answered, 'Fixing the wire, sir'. I asked, 'Isn't that a little unhealthy right about now?' He answered, 'Yes, sir, but the goddamned wire has to be fixed'. I asked, 'Don't those planes strafing the road bother you?' And he answered, 'No, sir, but you sure as hell do!'

Now, there was a real man. A real soldier. There was a man who devoted all he had to his duty, no matter how seemingly insignificant his duty might appear at the time, no matter how great the odds. And you should have seen those trucks on the road to Tunisia. Those drivers were magnificent. All day and all night they rolled over those son-of-a-bitching roads, never stopping, never faltering from their course, with shells bursting all around them all of the time. We got through on good old American guts.

Many of those men drove for over forty consecutive hours. These men weren't combat men, but they were soldiers with a job to do. They did it, and in one hell of a way they did it. They were part of a team. Without team effort, without them, the fight would have been lost. All of the links in the chain pulled together and the chain became unbreakable.

Don't forget, you men don't know that I'm here. No mention of that fact is to be made in any letters. The world is not supposed to know what the hell happened to me. I'm not supposed to be commanding this army. I'm not even supposed to be here in England. Let the first bastards to find out be the goddamned Germans. Someday I want to see them raise up on their piss-soaked hind legs and howl, 'Jesus Christ, it's the goddamned Third Army again and that son-of-a-f***ing-bitch Patton'.

We want to get the hell over there. The quicker we clean up this goddamned mess, the quicker we can take a little jaunt against the purple pissing Japs and clean out their nest, too. Before the goddamned Marines get all of the credit.

Sure, we want to go home. We want this war over with. The quickest way to get it over with is to go get the bastards who started it. The quicker they are whipped, the quicker we can go home. The shortest way home is through Berlin and Tokyo. And when we get to Berlin, I am personally going to shoot that paper-hanging son-of-a-bitch Hitler. Just like I'd shoot a snake!

When a man is lying in a shell hole, if he just stays there all day, a German will get to him eventually. The hell with that idea. The hell with taking it. My men don't dig foxholes. I don't want them to. Foxholes only slow up an offensive. Keep moving. And don't give the enemy time to dig one either. We'll win this war, but we'll win it only by fighting and by showing the Germans that we've got more guts than they have; or ever will have. We're not going to just shoot the sons-of-bitches, we're going to rip out their living goddamned guts and use them to grease the treads of our tanks. We're going to murder those lousy Hun c***suckers by the bushel-f***ing-basket.

War is a bloody, killing business. You've got to spill their blood, or they will spill yours. Rip them up the belly. Shoot them in the guts. When shells are hitting all around you and you wipe the dirt off your face and realise that instead of dirt it's the blood and guts of what once was your best friend beside you, you'll know what to do! I don't want to get any messages saying, 'I am holding my position'. We are not holding a goddamned thing. Let the Germans do that. We are advancing constantly and we are not interested in holding onto anything, except the enemy's balls. We are going to twist his balls and kick the living s*** out of him all of the time. Our basic plan of operation is to advance and to keep on advancing regardless of whether we have to go over, under, or through the enemy. We are going to go through him like crap through a goose; like s*** through a tin horn!

From time to time there will be some complaints that we are pushing our people too hard. I don't give a good goddamn about such complaints. I believe in the old and sound rule that an ounce of sweat will save a gallon of blood. The harder WE push, the more Germans we will kill. The more Germans we kill, the fewer of our men will be killed. Pushing means fewer casualties. I want you all to remember that.

There is one great thing that you men will all be able to say after this war is over and you are home once again. You may be thankful that twenty years from now when you are sitting by the fireplace with your grandson on your knee and he asks you what you did in the great World War II, you won't have to cough, shift him to the other knee and say, 'Well, your Granddaddy shovelled s*** in Louisiana'. No, sir, you can look him straight in the eye and say, 'Son, your Granddaddy rode with the Great Third Army and a Son-of-a-Goddamned-Bitch named Georgie Patton!' That is all.

The Atom Bomb
Harry S. Truman, Potsdam, Germany, 25 July 1945

American president Harry Truman (1884–1972) made this diary entry while meeting Allied leaders at Potsdam. The atom bomb had just been tested, but had not yet been used on Hiroshima and Nagasaki. Truman states that it will be used only on military targets, but it was later dropped on heavily populated areas of little military significance. Debate raged over whether its use had been necessary; many argued that, had the Japanese been invited to observe the test in the desert, they would surely have surrendered. In 1963, ex-president Dwight Eisenhower, who in 1945 had been supreme commander of Allied forces, told *Newsweek* magazine:

> *I voiced to him [Secretary of War Henry L. Stimson] my grave misgivings, first on the basis of my belief that Japan was already defeated and that dropping the bomb was completely unnecessary, and secondly because I thought that our country should avoid*

shocking world opinion by the use of a weapon whose employment was, I thought, no longer mandatory as a measure to save American lives. It was my belief that Japan was at that very moment seeking some way to surrender with a minimum of loss of 'face' ... It wasn't necessary to hit them with that awful thing.

Fleet Admiral William D. Leahy, Chair of the Joint Chiefs of Staff, said that, by using the bomb, the United States had 'adopted an ethical standard common to the barbarians of the Dark Ages'. But many believed that its use was justified on the grounds that it brought the war to an instant halt.

We have discovered the most terrible bomb in the history of the world. It may be the fire destruction prophesied in the Euphrates Valley Era, after Noah and his fabulous Ark.

Anyway we 'think' we have found the way to cause a disintegration of the atom. An experiment in the New Mexico desert was startling—to put it mildly. Thirteen pounds [6 kilograms] of the explosive caused the complete disintegration of a steel tower 60 feet [18 metres] high, created

a crater 6 feet [1.8 metres] deep and 1200 feet [365 metres] in diameter, knocked over a steel tower half a mile away and knocked men down 10,000 yards [9150 metres] away. The explosion was visible for more than 200 miles [320 kilometres] and audible for 40 miles [64 kilometres] and more.

This weapon is to be used against Japan between now and August 10th. I have told the Secretary of War, Mr Stimson, to use it so that military objectives and soldiers and sailors are the target and not women and children. Even if the Japs are savages, ruthless, merciless and fanatic, we as the leader of the world for the common welfare cannot drop that terrible bomb on the old capital or the new.

He and I are in accord. The target will be a purely military one and we will issue a warning statement asking the Japs to surrender and save lives. I'm sure they will not do that, but we will have given them the chance. It is certainly a good thing for the world that Hitler's crowd or Stalin's did not discover this atomic bomb. It seems to be the most terrible thing ever discovered, but it can be made the most useful.

FIGHTING WORDS

'I know not with what weapons World War III will be fought, but World War IV will be fought with sticks and stones.'
Albert Einstein (1879–1955), German physicist

'That since wars begin in the minds of men, it is in the minds of men that the defences of peace must be constructed.'
United Nations Educational, Scientific and Cultural Organization (UNESCO) Constitution, 16 November 1945

'Let us not be deceived—we are today in the midst of a cold war. Our enemies are to be found abroad and at home.'
The first use of the term 'cold war', in a speech written by Herbert Bayard Swope for US statesman Bernard Mannes Baruch (1870–1965), 1947

'War may sometimes be a necessary evil. But no matter how necessary, it is always an evil, never a good. We will not learn how to live together in peace by killing each other's children.'
Jimmy Carter (b. 1924), US president, 2002

The Cuban Missile Crisis
John F. Kennedy, Washington, D.C., 22 October 1962

At 7 pm on 22 October 1962, President John F. Kennedy (1917–63) made this televised speech to inform Americans of a recent Soviet military build-up in Cuba that included the installation of nuclear missiles. He had learned of the build-up one week earlier, after seeing photos taken by an American spy plane over Cuba. Kennedy discussed military options with his brother Robert, the US Attorney General, and his top military aides, and decided to organise a trade embargo supported by a naval blockade of Cuba, rather than order an air strike.

In the address, Kennedy outlined the threat, announced the blockade and stated that the United States would consider any missile launched from Cuba as a Soviet attack on the United States. On 28 October, Soviet president Nikita Khrushchev said he would remove the missiles from Cuba; in exchange, Kennedy secretly agreed to remove all US missiles from the Soviet border in Turkey. The trade embargo remains in place, however.

The crisis is generally agreed to be the moment in which the Cold War came closest to escalating into a nuclear war.

Good evening my fellow citizens:

This Government, as promised, has maintained the closest surveillance of the Soviet military build-up on the island of Cuba. Within the past week, unmistakable evidence has established the fact that a series of offensive missile sites is now in preparation on that imprisoned island. The purpose of these bases can be none other than to provide a nuclear strike capability against the Western Hemisphere ...

This urgent transformation of Cuba into an important strategic base—by the presence of these large, long-range, and clearly offensive weapons of sudden mass destruction—constitutes an explicit threat to the peace and security of all the Americas, in flagrant and deliberate defiance of the Rio Pact of 1947, the traditions of this nation and hemisphere, the joint resolution of the 87th Congress, the Charter of the United Nations and my own public warnings to the Soviets on 4 and 13 September. This action also contradicts

the repeated assurances of Soviet spokesmen, both publicly and privately delivered, that the arms build-up in Cuba would retain its original defensive character, and that the Soviet Union had no need or desire to station strategic missiles on the territory of any other nation.

The size of this undertaking makes clear that it has been planned for some months ...

Neither the United States of America nor the world community of nations can tolerate deliberate deception and offensive threats on the part of any nation, large or small. We no longer live in a world where only the actual firing of weapons represents a sufficient challenge to a nation's security to constitute maximum peril. Nuclear weapons are so destructive and ballistic missiles are so swift, that any substantially increased possibility of their use or any sudden change in their deployment may well be regarded as a definite threat to peace.

For many years both the Soviet Union and the United States, recognising this fact, have deployed strategic nuclear weapons with great care, never upsetting the precarious status quo which insured that these weapons would not be used in the absence of some vital challenge. Our own strategic missiles have never been transferred to the territory of any other nation under a cloak of secrecy and deception; and our history—unlike that of the Soviets since the end of World War II—demonstrates that we have no desire to dominate or conquer any other nation or impose our system upon its people. Nevertheless, American citizens have become adjusted to living daily on the bull's-eye of Soviet missiles located inside the USSR or in submarines.

In that sense, missiles in Cuba add to an already clear and present danger—although it should be noted the nations of Latin America have never previously been subjected to a potential nuclear threat ...

Our policy has been one of patience and restraint, as befits a peaceful and powerful nation, which leads a worldwide alliance. We have been determined not to be diverted from our central concerns by mere irritants and fanatics. But now further action is required—and it is under way; and these actions may only be the beginning. We will not prematurely or unnecessarily risk the costs of worldwide nuclear war in which even the fruits of victory would be ashes in our mouth—but neither will we shrink from that risk at any time it must be faced.

Acting, therefore, in the defence of our own security and of the entire western hemisphere, and under the authority entrusted to me by the Constitution as endorsed by the resolution of the Congress, I have directed that the following initial steps be taken immediately:

First: To halt this offensive build-up, a strict quarantine on all offensive military equipment under shipment to Cuba is being initiated. All ships of any kind bound for Cuba from whatever nation or port will, if found to contain cargoes of offensive weapons, be turned back. This quarantine will be extended, if needed, to other types of cargo and carriers. We are not at this time, however, denying the necessities of life as the Soviets attempted to do in their Berlin blockade of 1948.

Second: I have directed the continued and increased close surveillance of Cuba and its military build-up. The foreign ministers of the OAS [Organization of American States], in their communiqué of October 6, rejected secrecy in such matters in this hemisphere. Should these offensive military preparations continue, thus increasing the threat to the hemisphere, further action will be justified. I have directed the armed forces to prepare for any eventualities; and I trust that in the interest of both the Cuban people and the Soviet technicians at the sites, the hazards to all concerned in continuing this threat will be recognised.

Third: It shall be the policy of this nation to regard any nuclear missile launched from Cuba against any nation in the Western Hemisphere as an attack by the Soviet Union on the United States, requiring a full retaliatory response upon the Soviet Union.

Fourth: As a necessary military precaution, I have reinforced our base at Guantanamo, evacuated today the dependents of our personnel there, and ordered additional military units to be on a standby alert basis.

Fifth: We are calling tonight for an immediate meeting of the Organ of Consultation under the Organization of American States, to consider this threat to hemispheric security and to invoke articles 6 and 8 of the Rio Treaty in support of all necessary action. The United Nations Charter allows for regional security arrangements—and the nations of this hemisphere decided long ago against the military presence of outside powers. Our other allies around the world have also been alerted.

Sixth: Under the Charter of the United Nations, we are asking tonight that an emergency meeting of the Security Council be convoked without delay to take action against this latest Soviet threat to world peace. Our resolution will call for the prompt dismantling and withdrawal of all offensive weapons in Cuba, under the supervision of UN observers, before the quarantine can be lifted.

Seventh and finally: I call upon Chairman Khrushchev to halt and eliminate this clandestine, reckless and provocative threat to world peace and to stable relations between our two nations. I call upon him further to abandon this course of world domination, and to join in an historic effort to end the perilous arms race and to transform the history of man ...

My fellow citizens: let no one doubt that this is a difficult and dangerous effort on which we have set out. No one can see precisely what course it will take or what costs or casualties will be incurred. Many months of sacrifice and self-discipline lie ahead—months in which our patience and our will will be tested—months in which many threats and denunciations will keep us aware of our dangers. But the greatest danger of all would be to do nothing ...

Our goal is not the victory of might, but the vindication of right—not peace at the expense of freedom, but both peace and freedom, here in this hemisphere, and, we hope, around the world. God willing, that goal will be achieved.

Thank you and good night.

'Our Cause Is Just'
Margaret Thatcher, London, 26 May 1982

Margaret Thatcher (b. 1925), UK prime minister from 1979 to 1990, delivered this speech to the Conservative Women's Conference during the 1982 war between Argentina and Britain over Argentina's occupation of the Falkland, South Georgia and Sandwich islands. The war began on 19 March 1982 and ended when Argentina surrendered on 14 June; 649 Argentines and 258 Britons died. The defeat discredited the Argentine military government and led to the restoration of civilian rule in 1983. Conversely, Thatcher, whose support had been dwindling before the war, was returned to power with an increased parliamentary majority. Both countries still claim sovereignty over the islands.

Madam Chairman.
Our conference takes place at a time when great and grave issues face our country. Our hearts and minds are focused on the South Atlantic. You have been debating defence policy at a time when

our fighting men are engaged in one of the most remarkable military operations in modern times.

We have sent an immensely powerful task force, more than 100 ships, and 27,000 sailors, marines, soldiers and airmen, some 8000 miles [13,000 kilometres] away in the South Atlantic.

In a series of measured and progressive steps, over the past weeks, our forces have tightened their grip of the Falkland Islands. They have retaken South Georgia. Gradually they have denied fresh supplies to the Argentine garrison.

Finally, by the successful landing at San Carlos Bay in the early hours of Friday morning, they have placed themselves in a position to retake the islands and reverse the illegal invasion by Argentina.

By the skill of our pilots, our sailors and those manning the Rapier missile on shore they have inflicted heavy losses on the Argentine Air Force—over fifty aircraft have been destroyed ...

We in Britain know the reality of war. We know its hazards and its dangers. We know the task that faces our fighting men. They are now established on the Falkland Islands with all the necessary supplies. Although they still face formidable problems in difficult terrain with a hostile climate, their morale is high …

Madam Chairman, the theme of this conference is 'Living with our Neighbours' and it may seem inappropriate to be debating such a thing when there was open conflict between Britain and Argentina, and the lives of young men on both sides are being lost. But the whole basis of our foreign and defence policy, and indeed of the international political order depends on the friendship of neighbours, co-operating with them and abiding by the rule of law.

These are the very things which the illegal invasion of the Falkland Islands, had it gone unchallenged, would have subverted and destroyed. The Falkland Islands are British. The Falkland Islanders are British. They don't want to be ruled by Argentina, as those pictures of the welcome given to British marines and soldiers showed more clearly than a thousand words …

There were those who said we should have accepted the Argentine invasion as a *fait accompli*. But Madam Chairman, whenever the rule of force rather than the rule of law is seen to succeed, the world moves a step closer to anarchy.

The older generation in our country, and generations before them, have made sacrifices so that we could be a free society and belong to a community of nations which seeks to resolve disputes by civilised means. Today it falls to us to bear the same responsibility, we shall not shirk it. What has happened since that day, eight weeks ago, is a matter of history—the history of a nation which rose instinctively to the needs of the occasion.

For decades, the peoples of the Falkland Islands had enjoyed peace—with freedom—peace with justice, peace with democracy. They are our people and let no one doubt our profound longing for peace. But that peace was shattered by a wanton act of armed aggression by Argentina in blatant violation of international law. And everything that has happened since has stemmed from the invasion by the military dictatorship of Argentina. And sometimes I feel people need reminding of that fact more often. We want peace restored. But we want it with the same freedom, justice and democracy that the Islanders previously enjoyed ...

We are the victims; they are the aggressors ...

We came to military action reluctantly. But when territory which has been British for almost 150 years is seized and occupied; when not only British land, but British citizens, are in the power of an aggressor; then we have to restore our rights and the rights of the Falkland Islanders ...

When their land was invaded and their homes were overrun, they naturally turned to us for help, and we, their fellow citizens, 8000 miles [13,000 kilometres] away in our own much larger island, could not and did not beg to be excused ...

Surely we, of all people, have learned the lesson of history: that to appease an aggressor is to invite aggression elsewhere, and on an ever-increasing scale.

Other voices—again only a few—have accused us of clinging to colonialism or even imperialism. Let us remind those who advance that argument that we British have a record second to none of leading colony after colony to freedom and independence. We cling not to colonialism but to self-determination of peoples everywhere.

Still others—again only a few—say we must not put at risk our investments and interests in

Latin America; that trade and commerce are too important to us to put in jeopardy some of the valuable markets of the world.

What would the Islanders, under the heel of the invader, say to that?

What kind of people would we be if, enjoying the birthright of freedom ourselves, we were to abandon British citizens for the sake of commercial gain? We would never do it. Now we are present in strength on the Falkland Islands. Our purpose is to repossess them and we shall persevere until that purpose is accomplished.

Madam Chairman, our cause is just ...

It is the cause of freedom and the rule of law.

It is the cause of support for the weak against aggression by the strong.

Let us then draw together in the name, not of jingoism, but of justice.

Finally, let our nation, as it has so often in the past, remind itself—and the world: 'Nought shall make us rue, If England to herself do rest but true' [William Shakespeare, *King John*, Act V, Scene 7].

FAMOUS LAST WORDS

'No, you certainly can't.'
John F. Kennedy (1917–63), US president, replying to Nellie Connally, wife of Texas governor John Connally, who had said: 'You certainly can't say that the people of Dallas haven't given you a nice welcome, Mr President'. Seconds later, Kennedy was shot dead.

'Oh, I am so bored with it all.'
Winston Churchill (1874–1965), British statesman, before lapsing into a coma and dying nine days later

'Let's cool it brothers …'
Malcolm X (1925–65), African-American leader, to his three assassins

'I know you are here to kill me. Shoot, coward, you are only going to kill a man.'
Che Guevara (1928–67), Argentine Marxist revolutionary and Cuban guerrilla leader

'Don't worry, relax!'
Rajiv Gandhi (1944–91), Indian prime minister, to his staff just before being killed by a suicide bomber

Attack on Iraq
George Bush Sr, Washington, D.C.,
16 January 1991

This televised speech by George Bush Sr (b. 1924) was made two hours after the US and Coalition forces launched a major attack, dubbed 'Desert Storm', against Iraq. In August 1990, Iraqi forces had invaded oil-rich Kuwait, which had asked for the United States to come to its aid. The UN Security Council instigated a trade and financial embargo against Iraq, and on 29 November authorised the use of 'all necessary means' to oust Iraqi troops if they had not retreated by 15 January 1991.

Iraq did not believe that the United States, its recent ally in a war against neighbouring Iran, would use military force. But the Allied attack started the day after the deadline expired. Iraq was expelled from Kuwait; however, Iraqi leader Saddam Hussein held on to power in Iraq until March 2003, when a US-led coalition launched another invasion. Bush's approval ratings briefly soared after the war, but he was nonetheless defeated by Democrat candidate Bill Clinton in the 1992 presidential election.

Just two hours ago, Allied air forces began an attack on military targets in Iraq and Kuwait. These attacks continue as I speak. Ground forces are not engaged. This conflict started August 2, when the dictator of Iraq invaded a small and helpless neighbour. Kuwait, a member of the Arab League and a member of the United Nations, was crushed, its people brutalised. Five months ago, Saddam Hussein started this cruel war against Kuwait; tonight, the battle has been joined.

This military action, taken in accord with United Nations resolutions and with the consent of the United States Congress, follows months of constant and virtually endless diplomatic activity on the part of the United Nations, the United States and many, many other countries.

Arab leaders sought what became known as an Arab solution, only to conclude that Saddam Hussein was unwilling to leave Kuwait. Others travelled to Baghdad in a variety of efforts to restore peace and justice. Our Secretary of State, James Baker, held an historic meeting in Geneva, only to be totally rebuffed.

This past weekend, in a last-ditch effort, the Secretary General of the United Nations went to the Middle East with peace in his heart—his second such mission. And he came back from Baghdad with no progress at all in getting Saddam Hussein to withdraw from Kuwait.

Now, the twenty-eight countries with forces in the Gulf area have exhausted all reasonable efforts to reach a peaceful resolution, and have no choice but to drive Saddam from Kuwait by force. We will not fail.

As I report to you, air attacks are under way against military targets in Iraq. We are determined to knock out Saddam Hussein's nuclear bomb potential. We will also destroy his chemical weapons facilities. Much of Saddam's artillery and tanks will be destroyed. Our operations are designed to best protect the lives of all the Coalition forces by targeting Saddam's vast military arsenal ...

Our objectives are clear: Saddam Hussein's forces will leave Kuwait. The legitimate government of Kuwait will be restored to its rightful place, and Kuwait will once again be free.

Iraq will eventually comply with all relevant United Nations resolutions, and then, when peace is restored, it is our hope that Iraq will live as a peaceful and co-operative member of the family of nations, thus enhancing the security and stability of the Gulf.

Some may ask, why act now? Why not wait? The answer is clear. The world could wait no longer. Sanctions, though having some effect, showed no signs of accomplishing their objective. Sanctions were tried for well over five months, and we and our allies concluded that sanctions alone would not force Saddam from Kuwait.

While the world waited, Saddam Hussein systematically raped, pillaged and plundered a tiny nation no threat to his own. He subjected the people of Kuwait to unspeakable atrocities, and among those, maimed and murdered innocent children.

While the world waited, Saddam sought to add to the chemical weapons arsenal and he now possesses an infinitely more dangerous weapon of mass destruction—a nuclear weapon. And while the world waited, while the world talked peace and withdrawal, Saddam Hussein dug in and moved massive forces into Kuwait.

While the world waited, while Saddam stalled, more damage was being done to the fragile economies of the Third World, emerging democracies of Eastern Europe, to the entire world, including to our own economy.

The United States, together with the United Nations, exhausted every means at our disposal to bring this crisis to a peaceful end. However, Saddam clearly felt that by stalling and threatening and defying the United Nations, he could weaken the forces arrayed against him.

While the world waited, Saddam Hussein met every overture of peace with open contempt.

While the world prayed for peace, Saddam prepared for war.

I had hoped that when the United States Congress, in historic debate, took its resolute action, Saddam would realise he could not prevail, and would move out of Kuwait in accord with the United Nations resolutions. He did not do that. Instead, he remained intransigent, certain that time was on his side.

Saddam was warned over and over again to comply with the will of the United Nations: leave Kuwait or be driven out. Saddam has arrogantly rejected all warnings. Instead, he tried to make this a dispute between Iraq and the United States of America.

Well, he failed. Tonight twenty-eight nations—countries from five continents, Europe and Asia, Africa and the Arab League—have forces in the Gulf area standing shoulder-to-shoulder against Saddam Hussein. These countries had hoped the use of force could be avoided. Regrettably, we now believe that only force will make him leave.

Prior to ordering our forces into battle, I instructed our military commanders to take every necessary step to prevail, as quickly as possible, and with the greatest degree of protection possible for American and Allied servicemen and -women.

I've told the American people before that this will not be another Vietnam, and I repeat this here tonight. Our troops will have the best possible support in the entire world, and they will not be asked to fight with one hand tied behind their back. I'm hopeful that this fighting will not go on for long, and that casualties will be held to an absolute minimum.

This is an historic moment. We have in this past year made great progress in ending the long era of conflict and cold war. We have before us the opportunity to forge for ourselves and for future generations a new world order, a world where the rule of law, not the law of the jungle, governs the conduct of nations.

When we are successful, and we will be, we have a real chance at this new world order, an order in which a credible United Nations can use its peacekeeping role to fulfil the promise and vision of the UN's founders.

We have no argument with the people of Iraq. Indeed, for the innocents caught in this conflict, I pray for their safety.

Our goal is not the conquest of Iraq. It is the liberation of Kuwait. It is my hope that somehow the Iraqi people can, even now, convince their dictator that he must lay down his arms, leave Kuwait, and let Iraq itself rejoin the family of peace-loving nations.

Thomas Paine wrote many years ago: 'These are the times that try men's souls'. Those well-known words are so very true today. But even as planes of the multinational forces attack Iraq, I prefer to think of peace, not war. I am convinced not only that we will prevail, but that out of the horror of combat will come the recognition that no nation can stand against a world united. No nation will be permitted to brutally assault its neighbour.

No president can easily commit our sons and daughters to war. They are the nation's finest. Ours is an all-volunteer force, magnificently trained, highly motivated. The troops know why they're there. And listen to what they say, because they've said it better than any president or prime minister ever could.

Listen to 'Hollywood' Huddleston, Marine lance corporal. He says: 'Let's free these people so we can go home and be free again'.

And he's right. The terrible crimes and tortures committed by Saddam's henchmen against the innocent people of Kuwait are an affront to mankind and a challenge to the freedom of all.

Listen to one of our great officers out there, Marine Lieutenant General Walter Boomer: 'There are things worth fighting for. A world in which brutality and lawlessness are allowed to go unchecked isn't the kind of world we're going to want to live in'.

Listen to Master Sergeant J.P. Kendall of the Eighty-Second Airborne: 'We're here for more than just the price of a gallon of gas. What we're doing is going to chart the future of the world for the next hundred years. It's better to deal with this guy now than five years from now'.

And finally, we should all sit up and listen to Jackie Jones, an army lieutenant, when she says: 'If we let him get away with this, who knows what's going to be next'.

I've called upon Hollywood and Walter and J.P. and Jackie, and all their courageous comrades-in-arms, to do what must be done. Tonight, America and the world are deeply grateful to them and to their families.

And let me say to everyone listening or watching tonight: when the troops we've sent in finish their work, I'm determined to bring them home as soon as possible. Tonight, as our forces fight, they and their families are in our prayers.

May God bless each and every one of them, and the coalition forces at our side in the Gulf, and may He continue to bless our nation, the United States of America.

FIGHTING WORDS

'Politics is war without bloodshed, while war is politics with bloodshed.'
Mao Zedong (1893–1976), leader of China from 1949 until his death in 1976, 1938

'Mankind must put an end to war before war puts an end to mankind.'
John F. Kennedy (1917–63), US president, 1961

'Either war is obsolete or men are.'
R. Buckminster Fuller (1895–1983), US architect, author and inventor, 1966

'If it's natural to kill, how come men have to go into training to learn how?'
Joan Baez (b. 1941), US singer, songwriter and campaigner for peace and human rights, 1968

'It doesn't take a hero to order men into battle. It takes a hero to be one of those men who goes into battle.'
Norman Schwarzkopf Jr (b. 1934), US general, 1991 Gulf War

'Freedom from Fear'
Rudy Giuliani, New York, 1 October 2001

Lawyer and politician Rudy Giuliani (b. 1944) was the Republican mayor of New York at the time of the September 11 attacks. His approval rating had been dismal, but it skyrocketed as he displayed what was seen as strong leadership in the aftermath of the tragedy, including this speech to the UN General Assembly. *Time* magazine honoured him as its 2001 'Person of the Year', while the British government awarded him an honorary knighthood in February 2002. Since leaving office in late 2001, he has been much in demand on the speakers' circuit.

On September 11th, 2001, New York City—the most diverse city in the world—was viciously attacked in an unprovoked act of war. More than 5000 innocent men, women and children of every race, religion and ethnicity are lost. Among these were people from 80 different nations. To their representatives here today, I offer my condolences to you as well as on behalf of all New Yorkers who share this loss with you. This

was the deadliest terrorist attack in history. It claimed more lives than Pearl Harbor or D-Day.

This was not just an attack on the city of New York or on the United States of America. It was an attack on the very idea of a free, inclusive and civil society.

It was a direct assault on the founding principles of the United Nations itself. The Preamble to the UN Charter states that this organisation exists 'to reaffirm faith in fundamental human rights, in the dignity and worth of the human person … to practise tolerance and live together in peace as good neighbours [and] to unite our strength to maintain international peace and security'.

Indeed, this vicious attack places in jeopardy the whole purpose of the United Nations.

Terrorism is based on the persistent and deliberate violation of fundamental human rights. With bullets and bombs—and now with hijacked airplanes—terrorists deny the dignity of human life. Terrorism preys particularly on cultures and communities that practise openness and tolerance. Their targeting of innocent civilians mocks the efforts of those who seek to live together in peace as neighbours. It defies the very notion of being a neighbour.

This massive attack was intended to break our spirit. It has not done that. It has made us stronger, more determined and more resolved.

The bravery of our firefighters, our police officers, our emergency workers and civilians we may never learn of, in saving over 25,000 lives that day—carrying out the most effective rescue operation in our history—inspires all of us ...

The strength of America's response, please understand, flows from the principles upon which we stand.

Americans are not a single ethnic group.

Americans are not of one race or one religion.

Americans emerge from all your nations.

We are defined as Americans by our beliefs—not by our ethnic origins, our race or our religion. Our beliefs in religious freedom, political freedom and economic freedom—that's what makes an American. Our belief in democracy, the rule of law and respect for human life—that's how you become an American. It is these very principles—and the opportunities these principles give to so many to create a

better life for themselves and their families—
that make America, and New York, a 'shining
city on a hill' ...

It is tragic and perverse that it is because of
these very principles—particularly our religious,
political and economic freedoms—that we find
ourselves under attack by terrorists.

Our freedom threatens them, because they
know that if our ideas of freedom gain a foothold
among their people it will destroy their power.
So they strike out against us to keep those ideas
from reaching their people ...

The terrorists have no ideas or ideals with
which to combat freedom and democracy.
So their only defence is to strike out against
innocent civilians, destroying human life in
massive numbers and hoping to deter all of us
from our pursuit and expansion of freedom.

But the long-term deterrent of spreading our
ideals throughout the world is just not enough,
and may never be realised, if we do not act—and
act together—to remove the clear and present
danger posed by terrorism and terrorists.

The United Nations must hold accountable
any country that supports or condones

terrorism, otherwise you will fail in your primary mission as peacekeeper.

It must ostracise any nation that supports terrorism.

It must isolate any nation that remains neutral in the fight against terrorism.

Now is the time, in the words of the UN Charter, 'to unite our strength to maintain international peace and security'. This is not a time for further study or vague directives. The evidence of terrorism's brutality and inhumanity—of its contempt for life and the concept of peace—is lying beneath the rubble of the World Trade Center ...

Look at that destruction, that massive, senseless, cruel loss of human life and then I ask you to look in your hearts and recognise that there is no room for neutrality on the issue of terrorism. You're either with civilisation or with terrorists.

On one side is democracy, the rule of law and respect for human life; on the other is tyranny, arbitrary executions and mass murder.

We're right and they're wrong. It's as simple as that. And by that I mean that America and its allies are right about democracy, about religious, political and economic freedom.

The terrorists are wrong, and in fact evil, in their mass destruction of human life in the name of addressing alleged injustices ...

On this issue—terrorism—the United Nations must draw a line. The era of moral relativism between those who practise or condone terrorism, and those nations who stand up against it, must end. Moral relativism does not have a place in this discussion and debate ...

From the first day of this attack, an attack on New York and America, and I believe an attack on the basic principles that underlie this organisation, I have told the people of New York that we should not allow this to divide us, because then we would really lose what this city is all about. We have very strong and vibrant Arab and Muslim communities in New York City. They are an equally important part of the life of our city. We respect their religious beliefs. We respect everybody's religious beliefs—that's what America's about, that's what New York City is about. I have urged New Yorkers not to engage in any form of group blame or group hatred. This is exactly the evil that we are confronting with these terrorists.

And if we are going to prevail over terror, our ideals, principles and values must transcend all forms of prejudice. This is a very important part of the struggle against terrorism ...

Freedom from fear is a basic human right. We need to reassert our right to live free from fear with greater confidence and determination than ever before, here in New York City, across America and around the world. With one clear voice, unanimously, we need to say that we will not give in to terrorism.

Surrounded by our friends of every faith, we know that this is not a clash of civilisations; it is a conflict between murderers and humanity.

This is not a question of retaliation or revenge. It is a matter of justice leading to peace. The only acceptable result is the complete and total eradication of terrorism.

New Yorkers are strong and resilient. We are unified. And we will not yield to terror. We do not let fear make our decisions for us.

We choose to live in freedom.

'A Turning Point in History'
Tony Blair, Brighton, England, 2 October 2001

This powerful speech to the annual Labour Party Conference was the response of the British prime minister, Tony Blair (b. 1953), to the September 11 attacks. In fifty-four minutes, he set out a persuasive case for military action against Afghanistan's Taliban government, which supported al'Qaeda and its attacks on the United States and its allies. In the speech, Blair argues that inaction would be much more dangerous than action, and that terrorism must be fought worldwide at all military and governmental levels. He rebuts many of his critics' arguments and concludes with a call for a new, more vigorous approach to the world's problems.

In retrospect, the Millennium marked only a moment in time. It was the events of September 11 that marked a turning point in history, where we confront the dangers of the future and assess the choices facing humankind. It was a tragedy. An act of evil. From this nation, goes our deepest

sympathy and prayers for the victims and our profound solidarity with the American people. We were with you at the first. We will stay with you to the last.

Just two weeks ago, in New York, after the church service I met some of the families of the British victims. It was in many ways a very British occasion. Tea and biscuits. It was raining outside. Around the edge of the room, strangers making small talk, trying to be normal people in an abnormal situation. And as you crossed the room, you felt the longing and sadness; hands clutching photos of sons and daughters, wives and husbands; imploring you to believe them when they said there was still an outside chance of their loved ones being found alive, when you knew in truth that all hope was gone.

And then a middle-aged mother looks you in the eyes and tells you her only son has died, and asks you: why? I tell you: you do not feel like the most powerful person in the country at times like that. Because there is no answer. There is no justification for their pain. Their son did nothing wrong. The woman, seven months pregnant, whose child will never know its father, did nothing wrong. They don't want revenge. They want something better in memory of their loved ones.

I believe their memorial can and should be greater than simply the punishment of the guilty. It is that out of the shadow of this evil, should emerge lasting good: destruction of the machinery of terrorism wherever it is found; hope amongst all nations of a new beginning where we seek to resolve differences in a calm and ordered way; greater understanding between nations and between faiths; and above all justice and prosperity for the poor and dispossessed, so that people everywhere can see the chance of a better future through the hard work and creative power of the free citizen, not the violence and savagery of the fanatic ...

What happened on 11 September was without parallel in the bloody history of terrorism. Within a few hours, up to 7000 people were annihilated, the commercial centre of New York was reduced to rubble and in Washington and Pennsylvania further death and horror on an unimaginable scale. Let no one say this was a blow for Islam when the blood of innocent Muslims was shed along with those of the Christian, Jewish and other faiths around the world.

We know those responsible. In Afghanistan are scores of training camps for the export of terror. Chief amongst the sponsors and organisers is Osama bin Laden. He is supported, shielded and given succour by the Taliban regime. Two days before the 11 September attacks, Masood, the leader of the opposition Northern Alliance, was assassinated by two suicide bombers. Both were linked to bin Laden. Some may call that coincidence. I call it payment—payment in the currency these people deal in: blood. Be in no doubt: bin Laden and his people organised this atrocity. The Taliban aid and abet him. He will not desist from further acts of terror. They will not stop helping him. Whatever the dangers of the action we take, the dangers of inaction are far, far greater.

Look for a moment at the Taliban regime. It is undemocratic. That goes without saying. There is no sport allowed, or television or photography. No art or culture is permitted. All other faiths, all other interpretations of Islam are ruthlessly suppressed. Those who practise their faith are imprisoned. Women are treated in a way almost too revolting to be credible. First driven out of university; girls not allowed to go to school; no legal rights; unable to go out of doors without a man. Those that disobey are stoned. There is now no contact permitted with Western agencies, even those delivering food. The people live in abject poverty. It is a regime founded on fear and funded on the drugs trade. The biggest drugs hoard in the world is in Afghanistan, controlled by the Taliban. Ninety per cent of the heroin on British streets originates in Afghanistan. The arms the Taliban are buying today are paid for with the lives of young British people buying their drugs on British streets. That is another part of their regime that we should seek to destroy.

So what do we do? Don't overreact some say. We aren't. We haven't lashed out. No missiles on the first night just for effect. Don't kill innocent people. We are not the ones who waged war on the innocent. We seek the guilty. Look for a diplomatic solution. There is no diplomacy with bin Laden or the Taliban regime. State an ultimatum and get their response. We stated the ultimatum; they haven't responded. Understand the causes of terror. Yes, we should try, but let there be no moral ambiguity about this: nothing could ever justify the events of 11 September, and it is to turn justice on its head to pretend it could. The action we take will be proportionate; targeted; we will do all we humanly can to avoid civilian casualties.

But understand what we are dealing with. Listen to the calls of those passengers on the planes. Think of the children on them, told they were going to die. Think of the cruelty beyond our comprehension as amongst the screams and the anguish of the innocent, those hijackers drove at full throttle planes laden with fuel into buildings where tens of thousands worked. They have no moral inhibition on the slaughter of the innocent. If they could have murdered not 7000 but 70,000 does anyone doubt they would have done so and rejoiced in it? There is no compromise possible with such people, no meeting of minds, no point of understanding with such terror. Just a choice: defeat it or be defeated by it. And defeat it we must.

Any action taken will be against the terrorist network of bin Laden ...

Here in this country and in other nations round the world, laws will be changed, not to deny basic liberties but to prevent their abuse and protect the most basic liberty of all: freedom from terror. New extradition laws will be introduced; new rules to ensure asylum is not a front for terrorist entry. This country is proud of its tradition in giving asylum to those fleeing tyranny. We will always do so. But we have a duty to protect the system from abuse. It must be overhauled radically so that from now on, those who abide by the rules get help and those that don't, can no longer play the system to gain unfair advantage over others ...

In all of this, at home and abroad, the same beliefs throughout: that we are a community of people, whose self-interest and mutual interest at crucial points merge, and that it is through a sense of justice that community is born and nurtured. And what does this concept of justice consist of? Fairness, people all of equal worth, of course. But also reason and tolerance. Justice has no favourites; not amongst nations, peoples or faiths. When we act to bring to account those that committed the atrocity of September 11, we do so, not out of bloodlust.

We do so because it is just. We do not act against Islam. The true followers of Islam are our brothers and sisters in this struggle. Bin Laden is no more obedient to the proper teaching of the Koran than those Crusaders of the twelfth century who pillaged and murdered, represented the teaching of the Gospel. It is time the west confronted its ignorance of Islam. Jews, Muslims and Christians are all children of Abraham. This is the moment to bring the faiths closer together in understanding of our common values and heritage, a source of unity and strength. It is time also for parts of Islam to confront prejudice against America and not only Islam but parts of Western societies too …

So I believe this is a fight for freedom. And I want to make it a fight for justice too. Justice not only to punish the guilty. But justice to bring those same values of democracy and freedom to people round the world. And I mean: freedom, not only in the narrow sense of personal liberty but in the broader sense of each individual having the economic and social freedom to develop their potential to the full. That is what community means, founded on the equal worth of all. The starving, the wretched, the dispossessed, the ignorant, those living in want and squalor from the deserts of Northern Africa to the slums of Gaza, to the mountain ranges of Afghanistan: they too are our cause.

This is a moment to seize. The kaleidoscope has been shaken. The pieces are in flux. Soon they will settle again. Before they do, let us reorder this world around us. Today, humankind has the science and technology to destroy itself or to provide prosperity to all. Yet science can't make that choice for us. Only the moral power of a world, acting as a community, can. 'By the strength of our common endeavour we achieve more together than we can alone.' For those people who lost their lives on September 11 and those that mourn them: now is the time for the strength to build that community. Let that be their memorial.

FIGHTING TALK IN THE TWENTY-FIRST CENTURY

Fighting talk of all kinds continues to be created in the twenty-first century. As political and military alliances chop and change, we invent neologisms to explain why last week's 'terrorist' is this week's 'freedom fighter'. 'Spin doctors' have brought us such vile euphemisms as 'collateral damage' (death of innocent noncombatants), 'friendly fire' (our weapons that kill our forces), 'rendition' (torture), 'targets' (people we want to kill), 'ethnic cleansing' (mass murder); and dysphemisms such as 'terrorist' (anyone who disagrees with us and uses force). 'Weapons of mass destruction' has been further euphemised into 'WMD', much as Kentucky Fried Chicken disappeared in favour of 'KFC', and for a similar reason—people are more likely to buy it.

Fighting talk has even invaded other spheres. In medicine, we 'fight off' a cold with a 'shot' of medicine or perhaps a 'magic bullet'. In commerce we 'fight' for market share, engage in a 'price war' or 'launch' a corporate 'raid' on another company. And in information technology if someone 'hacks' into our computer, we may be 'attacked' by a virus.

'Axis of Evil'
George W. Bush, Washington, D.C., 29 January 2002

In this State of the Union speech, George W. Bush (b. 1946) asserts that an 'axis of evil' comprising North Korea, Iraq and Iran is jeopardising 'the peace of the world'. He sets out what would become known as 'the Bush doctrine'—that the 'war on terror' justifies a preventative invasion where a threat to the US is perceived.

The speech was roundly criticised, by friend and foe alike. North Korean state television dubbed Bush a 'nuclear maniac'; Iranian president Khatami said Bush was 'warmongering' and 'insulting'; and Iraqi vice president Taha Yassin Ramadan called Bush's comments 'stupid' and 'inappropriate'. None of this was surprising, but British foreign secretary Jack Straw stated that Bush's remarks were designed to increase his domestic standing before looming congressional elections, rather than identify a plausible danger. French foreign minister Hubert Védrine labelled Bush's approach 'simplistic', and Chris Patten, the British politician in charge of the European Union's external relations, said the speech was 'unhelpful' and 'more rhetoric than substance'.

Shortly after delivering this speech, Bush began claiming—wrongly, as it turned out—that Iraq was involved in the September 11 attacks, an inaccuracy that was used to help justify the 2003 American-led invasion of Iraq.

As we gather tonight, our nation is at war, our economy is in recession, and the civilised world faces unprecedented dangers. Yet the state of our Union has never been stronger.

We last met in an hour of shock and suffering. In four short months, our nation has comforted the victims, begun to rebuild New York and the Pentagon, rallied a great coalition, captured, arrested and rid the world of thousands of terrorists, destroyed Afghanistan's terrorist training camps, saved a people from starvation, and freed a country from brutal oppression.

The American flag flies again over our embassy in Kabul. Terrorists who once occupied Afghanistan now occupy cells at Guantanamo

Bay. And terrorist leaders who urged followers to sacrifice their lives are running for their own.

America and Afghanistan are now allies against terror. We'll be partners in rebuilding that country ...

The last time we met in this chamber, the mothers and daughters of Afghanistan were captives in their own homes, forbidden from working or going to school. Today women are free, and are part of Afghanistan's new government. And we welcome the new Minister of Women's Affairs, Doctor Sima Samar.

Our progress is a tribute to the spirit of the Afghan people, to the resolve of our coalition, and to the might of the United States military. When I called our troops into action, I did so with complete confidence in their courage and skill. And tonight, thanks to them, we are winning the war on terror. The men and women of our Armed Forces have delivered a message now clear to every enemy of the United States: even 7000 miles [11,000 kilometres] away, across oceans and continents, on mountaintops and in caves—you will not escape the justice of this nation ...

What we have found in Afghanistan confirms that, far from ending there, our war against terror is only beginning. Most of the 19 men who hijacked planes on September the 11th were trained in Afghanistan's camps, and so were tens of thousands of others. Thousands of dangerous killers, schooled in the methods of murder, often supported by outlaw regimes, are now spread throughout the world like ticking time bombs, set to go off without warning.

Thanks to the work of our law enforcement officials and coalition partners, hundreds of terrorists have been arrested. Yet, tens of thousands of trained terrorists are still at large. These enemies view the entire world as a battlefield, and we must pursue them wherever they are. So long as training camps operate, so long as nations harbour terrorists, freedom is at risk. And America and our allies must not, and will not, allow it.

Our nation will continue to be steadfast and patient and persistent in the pursuit of two great objectives. First, we will shut down terrorist camps, disrupt terrorist plans and bring terrorists to justice. And, second, we must prevent the terrorists and regimes who seek chemical, biological or nuclear weapons from threatening the United States and the world …

My hope is that all nations will heed our call, and eliminate the terrorist parasites who threaten their countries and our own. Many nations are acting forcefully. Pakistan is now cracking down on terror, and I admire the strong leadership of President Musharraf.

But some governments will be timid in the face of terror. And make no mistake about it: if they do not act, America will.

Our second goal is to prevent regimes that sponsor terror from threatening America or our friends and allies with weapons of mass destruction. Some of these regimes have been pretty quiet since September 11. But we know their true nature. North Korea is a regime arming with missiles and weapons of mass destruction, while starving its citizens.

Iran aggressively pursues these weapons and exports terror, while an unelected few repress the Iranian people's hope for freedom.

Iraq continues to flaunt its hostility toward America and to support terror. The Iraqi regime has plotted to develop anthrax, and nerve gas, and nuclear weapons for over a decade. This is a regime that has already used poison gas to murder thousands of its own citizens—leaving the bodies of mothers huddled over their dead children. This is a regime that agreed to international inspections—then kicked out the inspectors. This is a regime that has something to hide from the civilised world.

States like these, and their terrorist allies, constitute an axis of evil, arming to threaten the peace of the world. By seeking weapons of mass destruction, these regimes pose a grave and growing danger. They could provide these arms to terrorists, giving them the means to match their hatred. They could attack our allies or attempt to blackmail the United States. In any of these cases, the price of indifference would be catastrophic.

We will work closely with our coalition to deny terrorists and their state sponsors the materials, technology and expertise to make and deliver weapons of mass destruction. We will develop and deploy effective missile defences to protect America and our allies from sudden attack ... America will do what is necessary to ensure our nation's security.

We'll be deliberate, yet time is not on our side. I will not wait on events, while dangers gather. I will not stand by, as peril draws closer and closer. The United States of America will not permit the world's most dangerous regimes to threaten us with the world's most destructive weapons.

Our war on terror is well begun, but it is only begun. This campaign may not be finished on our watch—yet it must be and it will be waged on our watch.

We can't stop short. If we stop now— leaving terror camps intact and terror states unchecked—our sense of security would be false and temporary. History has called America and our allies to action, and it is both our responsibility and our privilege to fight freedom's fight ...

The last time I spoke here, I expressed the hope that life would return to normal. In some ways, it has. In others, it never will. Those of us who have lived through these challenging times have been changed by them. We've come to know truths that we will never question: evil is real, and it must be opposed. Beyond all differences of race or creed, we are one country, mourning together and facing danger together. Deep in the American character, there is honour, and it is stronger than cynicism. And many have discovered again that even in tragedy—especially in tragedy—God is near.

In a single instant, we realised that this will be a decisive decade in the history of liberty, that we've been called to a unique role in human events. Rarely has the world faced a choice more clear or consequential.

Our enemies send other people's children on missions of suicide and murder. They embrace tyranny and death as a cause and a creed. We stand for a different choice, made long ago, on the day of our founding. We affirm it again today. We choose freedom and the dignity of every life.

Steadfast in our purpose, we now press on. We have known freedom's price. We have shown freedom's power. And in this great conflict, my fellow Americans, we will see freedom's victory.

Thank you all. May God bless.

FIGHTING SONG

Amazing Grace

Amazing grace, how sweet the sound,
That saved a wretch like me!
I once was lost but now am found,
Was blind, but now I see.

'Twas grace that taught my heart to fear,
And grace my fears relieved.
How precious did that grace appear
The hour I first believed.

Through many dangers, toils and snares
I have already come.
'Twas grace that brought me safe thus far
And grace will lead me home.

The Lord has promised good to me,
His word my hope secures.
He will my shield and portion be
As long as life endures.

Yes, when this flesh and heart shall fail,
And mortal life shall cease;
I shall possess, within the veil,
A life of joy and peace.

The earth shall soon dissolve like snow,
The sun forbear to shine;
But God, who called me here below,
Will be forever mine.

This much-loved Christian hymn was originally named 'Faith's Review and Expectation' and was written in 1772 by English priest and reformed slave-trafficker John Newton. The lyrics, which sum up the concept of divine grace, are based on 1 Chronicles 17:16–17. Newton had become a Christian following his apparently miraculous escape from a storm at sea.

The song has been an anthem for various civil-rights and peace movements, and is routinely sung at annual events held to commemorate the September 11 attacks. It is the very antithesis of fighting talk.

INDEX

A

Agincourt, Battle of 43–4
Alexius I Comnenus 34
'Amazing Grace' (song) 235–6
American Indians 75–6
Argentina 193–8
atom bomb 181–3

B

Baez, Joan 209
Bailly, Jean-Sylvain 48
Baruch, Bernard Mannes 184
Belgium 95, 129–31
Beowulf 27–8
Bertran de Born 39
bin Laden, Osama 220, 224
Blair, Tony 217–25
Booth, John Wilkes 69
Borodino, Battle of 62
Boudicca 25–6
Britain, Battle of 142, 166–8
Bush, George, Sr 200–8
Bush, George W. 227–34

C

Caesar, Julius 21
Callixtus III, Pope 40
Carter, Jimmy 184
Cataline, Lucius 22–4
Cavell, Edith 92
Chamberlain, Neville 115–6, 126–8, 138
Charles VII of France 40
Che Guevara 199
Churchill, Winston 129–42, 147–8, 158–9, 199
Clemenceau, Georges 92, 100
Connally, Nellie 199
Connor, Tommie 114
Council of Clermont 34–8
Creel, George 79
Crusades 33, 34–8
Cuban Missile Crisis 185–92
Curtin, John 158–68

D

Daladier, Édouard 115
Danton, Georges Jacques 48, 56–7
Drake, Francis 46

E

Edward the Confessor 29
Einstein, Albert 184
Eisenhower, Dwight 181–2
Elizabeth I of England 39, 45–7

F

Falkland Islands 193
'Four Minute Men' 79–85
French Revolution 48, 56–7
Fuller, R. Buckminster 209

G

Gandhi, Mohandas 169
Garibaldi, Giuseppe 63–5
Giuliani, Rudy 210–6
Goldman, Emma 86–91
Greco–Persian Wars 16–20
Greek mythology 10–1
Guantanamo 190, 228–9

H

Hale, Nathan 48
Hastings, Battle of 29–32, 33

Hemingway, Ernest 169
Henry, Patrick 49–55, 90
Henry V (Shakespeare) 43–4
Henry VI of England 40–2
Herodotus 16–20
Hindenburg, Paul von 97
Hitler, Adolf 97–112, 115–6, 126, 135, 143–9
Homer 10–4
Howard, General Oliver O. 75, 76
Hundred Years' War 40–4

I
India 106
Indonesia 160
Iran 227, 231–3
Iraq 200–8, 227–8, 231–3
Islam 34–8, 215, 219–20, 224

J
Japan 117, 125, 154–7, 158–68, 181–3
Joan of Arc 40–2
John of Salisbury 39
Joseph, Chief of Nez Perce 75–6

K
Kennedy, John F. 185–92, 199, 209
Key, Francis Scott 78
Khrushchev, Nikita 185, 191
Kuwait 200–8

L
'La Marseillaise' (anthem) 58–9
Leahy, William D. 182
Lee, Robert E. 68, 69
Leip, Hans 114
Lenin, Vladimir 96
'Lili Marlene' (song) 113–4
Lincoln, Abraham 66–7, 69–74, 164
Lloyd George, David 93–5

Louis XIV of France 48
Ludendorff, Erich von 92

M
McAdoo, William 81
Machiavelli, Niccolò 39
Malcolm X 199
Manouchian, Missak 153
Mao Zedong 209
Marie Antoinette 48
Massoud, Ahmed Shah 220
Menelaus of Sparta 12–4
Menzies, Robert 117–9
Miletus, Fall of 16–20
Molotov, Vyacheslav 150–2
Musharraf, President 231
Mussolini, Benito 115, 153

N
Napoleon Bonaparte 60–1, 62, 135, 151
National Socialism 97–112
Newton, John 236
North Korea 227, 231–3

P
Pacific War 156, 158–68
Pakistan 231
Patten, Chris 227–8
Patton, George S. 170–80
Pearl Harbor 125, 154–7
Philip II of Spain 45
Pisander 12–4
Pistoria, Battle of 22–4
Poland 118–9, 126–7, 145

R
Rankin, Jeannette 169
Roosevelt, Franklin D. 120–4, 154–7, 158–9
Russia 96, 125, 128, 138, 150–2, 185

S

Saddam Hussein 200–8
Saint Exupéry, Antoine de 169
Sartre, Jean-Paul 169
Scholl, Hans 153
Schultze, Norbert 114
Schwarzkopf Jr, Norman 209
September 11 210–25, 228, 230
Shakespeare, William 43–4, 198
Sherman, William T. 68
'Star-Spangled Banner' 77–8
Straw, Jack 227
Sun Tzu 21

T

Tacitus 25–6
Taliban 217, 220–1, 228–30
Talleyrand, Charles de 68

Thatcher, Margaret 193–8
Trojan War 10–4
Trotsky, Leon 153
Truman, Harry S. 181–3

U

United Nations 184, 191, 200, 211, 214
Urban, Pope 34–8
US Civil War 66–7, 69–74

W

War of American Independence 49–55, 66
Wilde, Oscar 68
Wilhelm II, Kaiser 92
William the Conqueror 29–32
Wilson, Woodrow 79, 81, 88–9

TEXT CREDITS

Adolf Hitler, speech to the Industry Club, Dusseldorf, Germany, 27 January 1932, © State of Bavaria, Germany, http://www.humanitas-international.org/showcase/chronography/speeches/1932-01-27.html

Adolf Hitler, 'Before the Gate of Germany Stands the New German Army', Nuremberg, Germany, 14 September 1936, © State of Bavaria, Germany, http://www.humanitas-international.org/showcase/chronography/speeches/1932-01-27.html

Hans Leip ©, 'Lili Marlene', written in 1915, Germany.

Adolf Hitler, 'We Are Merely Interested in Safeguarding Peace', Reichstag, Berlin, 4 May 1941, © State of Bavaria, Germany, http://www.humanitas-international.org/showcase/chronography/speeches/1932-01-27.html

Harry S. Truman ©, diary entry, 25 July 1945, reproduced with permission from the Harry S. Truman Library and Museum.

Margaret Thatcher ©, speech to the Conservative Women's Conference, London, 26 May 1982, reproduced with permission from the Margaret Thatcher Foundation, http://www.margaretthatcher.org

Tony Blair ©, address to the Labour Party Conference, 2 October 2001, Brighton, England, reproduced with permission from the Office of Tony Blair, www.tonyblairoffice.org

First published in 2010 by Pier 9, an imprint of Murdoch Books Pty Limited

Murdoch Books Australia
Pier 8/9, 23 Hickson Road
Millers Point NSW 2000
Phone: +61 (0) 2 8220 2000
Fax: +61 (0) 2 8220 2558
www.murdochbooks.com.au

Murdoch Books UK Limited
Erico House, 6th Floor North
93/99 Upper Richmond Road
Putney, London SW15 2TG
Phone: +44 (0) 20 8785 5995
Fax: +44 (0) 20 8785 5985
www.murdochbooks.co.uk

Publisher: Diana Hill
Project Manager: Paul O'Beirne
Editors: Sarah Baker, Scott Forbes
Design: Jenny Grigg

Commissioned text and design copyright © Murdoch Books Pty Limited 2010.
Text first published in *Fighting Talk* by James Inglis (Pier 9, 2008).

Every reasonable effort has been made to trace the owners of copyright materials in this book, but in some instances this has proven impossible. The author and publisher will be glad to receive information leading to more complete acknowledgements in subsequent printings of the book and in the meantime extend their apologies for any omissions.

All rights reserved. No part of this publication may be reproduced, stored in a retrieval system or transmitted in any form or by any means, electronic, mechanical photocopying, recording or otherwise without prior permission of the publisher.

National Library of Australia Cataloguing-in-Publication Data:

Title:	The war of words.
ISBN:	9781741967302 (pbk)
Series:	Pocket history series.
Notes:	Includes index.
Subjects:	Military history.
	Speeches, addresses, etc
	War and society—History.
	War—Psychological aspects.
Dewey Number:	355.009

A catalogue record for this book is available from the British Library.

Printed on FSC-accredited paper. Printed in China.